WHAT (

MW01232773

Kathy Taylor is every Sunday School teacher's dream: she soaks up every word. She not only soaks, she splashes! You, as the reader, will get drenched by her showers of blessing. You will love her research but you'll love her heart more.

Jane Lee Bateman
author, I WILL NEVER...
Conference speaker

Oh my goodness, Kathy's Splashes of God Light devotionals are so refreshing and inspiring. She has a different spin on each one, for example, there is a sheep having a conversation with us, just a delightful way of sharing. After all that's exactly what we are, sheep being led by the Master.

Debby Duncan

This author is personally connected to her Lord and God. She writes as a prophet of love, offering the reader visions of the holiness and majesty of God, which can be felt, tasted, and cherished, and which never diminish, no matter how many times you read it.

—Rebecca Raymond, RN

Katherine Taylor's devotional entitled "Get Lost" touched me so deeply. The morning that I read it, it felt as if she were looking into my very soul. That entire text, I felt, was meant especially for me and brought a clearer focus on my life.

Levonia Chambers, RMA

It is extraordinary how often this author's devotions seem "hand-picked" especially for me. The chaos of daily life may make it difficult to focus on God's Word but her devotions have helped me redirect my thoughts back to the Lord. Her verse selection together with her thought provoking comments guide my mind back to the Lord's will for my life.

—Reggie Scoggins, RN

This author has been blessed by God with a divine gift. Her words of devotion for her God should be shared with the world. With a writing style reminiscent of Max Lucado, the tenderness and sweetness of Christ brightly shines through, leaving you wanting more of Jesus.

—Lorie F. Grant, LPN

This book will lift your spirit and put some *Sonshine* in your day. I have been blessed by the content which truly reflects Christ.

—Rev Eddie Taylor, Swann Station Baptist Church, Sanford, NC

The tone of your manuscript is inspiring. It's a very positive manuscript that shares the message of the Bible. There is no judgment for nonbelievers, only the wish that they see that Jesus is the way to heaven. The manuscript is bathed with the author's happiness, and it is clearly the tone set for this manuscript that calls everyone to be part of Jesus's family.

—Germaine Canilao, Editor, Tate Publishing and Interprises, LLC

I LOVE TO TELL
THE STORY

*May this bless you
richly as you serve
our God —*

Kathy Shook Taylor

I LOVE TO TELL THE STORY

OF *JESUS AND HIS LOVE*

katherine shook taylor

TATE PUBLISHING
AND ENTERPRISES, LLC

Published by Tate Publishing & Enterprises, LLC
127 E. Trade Center Terrace | Mustang, Oklahoma 73064 USA
1.888.361.9473 | www.tatepublishing.com

Tate Publishing is committed to excellence in the publishing industry. The company reflects the philosophy established by the founders, based on Psalm 68:11,
"The Lord gave the word and great was the company of those who published it."

Book design copyright © 2013 by Tate Publishing, LLC. All rights reserved.
Cover design by Arjay Grecia
Interior design by Jake Muelle

Published in the United States of America

ISBN: 978-1-62902-978-8
1. Religion / Christian Life / Devotional
2. Religion / Christian Life / Personal Growth
13.11.01

I love to tell the story
of unseen things above,
of Jesus and his glory,
of Jesus and his love.
I love to tell the story,
because I know 'tis true;
it satisfies my longing
as nothing else can do.

I love to tell the story,
'twill be my theme in glory,
to tell the old, old story
of Jesus and his love.

I love to tell the story;
more wonderful it seems
than all the golden fancies
of all our golden dreams.
I love to tell the story,
it did so much for me;
and that is just the reason
I tell it now to thee.

I love to tell the story;
'tis pleasant to repeat
what seems, each time I tell it,
more wonderfully sweet.
I love to tell the story,
for some have never heard
the message of salvation
from God's own holy Word.

❧

I love to tell the story,
for those who know it best
seem hungering and thirsting
to hear it like the rest.
And when, in scenes of glory,
I sing the new, new song,
'twill be the old, old story
that I have loved so long.

—*Arabella Katherine Hankey 1866*
Public domain

DEDICATION

This book is lovingly dedicated to my precious father, Ernest Shook, who even today, at age 96, is still teaching me about the love of Jesus. He is a shining example of unconditional love to his three children. I have long been grateful to have been placed in his loving care.

Also to my mother, Grace, who is now at home with Christ. How I miss hearing her prayers in the middle of the night, laced with tears and tiptoeing in closer to see her kneeled at her bedside. She was *standing* in the gap for me.

To my, one of a kind big sister, Robbie, my other mother, and my loving and very protective big brother, Tommy. They were like having another set of parents!

To my dear husband, Michael, who was a great encourager for this special challenge. Thank you for cleaning the kitchen after dinner all those nights while urging me to write.

Most of all, this writing is dedicated to Jesus Christ, the Lover of my Soul. Lord, may you receive all glory and honor for without You, Father, I realize I could do nothing.

ACKNOWLEDGMENTS

This book is now complete because of the support of so many. I thank you all from the bottom of my heart.

Rebecca Raymond—You are my mentor and dear friend. You believed in me and the Splashes of God Light from the beginning, and I am forever grateful to you. Thank you for all of the imaginative conversations that we have shared and especially for the laughter in the halls of GCC.

Debby Duncan—You are the bubbliest and most encouraging cheerleader that one could hope for and my dear sister in Christ. No one could ever be discouraged around you. Thank you for sharing the joy!

Jane Bateman—My master teacher. Thank you for your love and support. You have taught me much!

Dana Lee—Here it is Dana!.... Finally. Thank you for each one of the ever-ready compliments and your sincere encouragement on a daily basis. You are precious to me.

Stacey Kindall—How could I have finished without all of the "you can do it, Margaret's" and your constant prayer for me? Thank you for every one of your sister hugs......

Reggie Scoggins—You are an inspiration to me, Reggie. I appreciate all of the love, support, hugs, and I am ever thankful that God led our paths together.

Patti Gowan—You are my long-time dear forever friend. Thank you for your prayers, our long conversations, for being my sounding board, and for sharing your son with me. We did pretty good, didn't we?

Curt Gowan—You are the best pseudo son that a Mama Kat could imagine. You have given me many years of joy. Thank you for loving Jesus as you do. A mother's dream.

Lorie Grant—My little *sister*, how I love you. Thank you so, so much for your encouraging words and your prayers. I am grateful for all of our years and forever memories together. Mostly, for our talks about our Lord. I look forward to sharing heaven with you!

Barbara Jackson—Barbie, thank you for being such a fan of and sharer of the Splashes. You have encouraged me more than you know. Thank you for helping me spread the Word.

Lynn Foster—You have long been my fearless leader. Thank you for making my e-mail devotionals possible and for being a forever sister-friend. Thank you, too, for all the laughs we have shared. You have made it a little easier to come to work, knowing you are here. I love you.

Crystal Humphries—You are a most precious friend to me. Everyone needs someone to confide in, share dreams with, as well as burdens. I am most blessed to have you for that friend, not to mention a little sister.

Tammy Pridmore—Your encouragement and prayer inspired me to make this happen.

Melodie W. Smith—You haven't a clue what you mean to me. Thank you for your unending support and being my forever friend. I will never forget you!

Lisa Kirby—My tiny effervescent angel! I so admire your bold love for our God.

Shannon Lanford—Shannon, I love your soft and gentle manner as well as your oft given encouragement. You are a jewel to me.

Vickie Newman—Noodle, thank you for your kind words and praise about the Splashes… I love you and our boys!

Heather Hinds—Heather, thank you for your kind endorsements of the Splashes. I cherish each one.

Theresa Sessions—My prayer partner and dear sister in Christ.

Asha Desai—I am so thankful for you. You are my precious and encouraging friend.

Melissa McCarter—yet another little sister. I am so blessed.

Levonia Chambers—I love your sweet spirit and appreciate your encouragement more than you can imagine.

Carole Gosnell—You are such an inspiration to me. Thank you for your prayers.

Tammy Clary—I cherish every one of your "Amen, Sister's" They have spurred me on.

Kelly Taber—Do you have any idea how you have encouraged me? I could never thank you enough.

Beth Sain—Your sweet compliments urged me to continue to share the "Good News"

Patsy Steadman—How special you are to me Patsy. I have loved you since the first day you came to work.

Donna Griffin—my friend who is full of laughter and encouragement, how I appreciate you!

Tate Publishing—Thank you for allowing me this grand opportunity and for your ever ready and helpful guidance. You are appreciated more than you could know.

Do you ever feel that no one loves you or understands you? That no one cares? Do you ever feel abandoned or alone? Then, I Love to Tell the Story, is written just for you, in wanting to help you, dear reader, to realize and completely understand the Love of our Living God for you, personally. You may be like I was as a young Christian…. I knew in my head that God loved me… I accepted it. I appreciated it… I loved Him back. But when I finally "got it" and realized the depth, fullness and completeness of His matchless Love and realized it in my heart, why, it changed my walk with Him. Our relationship grew sweeter, I longed to be with Him more every day. It deepened my relationship with Him. Won't you take time to explore for yourself the nature of God, Jesus and the Holy Spirit and personally experience this genuine Love that will never forsake you? You can trust Him. God so wants to reveal His great Love for you and be a part of your everyday life. He is knocking at the door of your heart, desiring to enter….Won't you invite Him in? I did, and let me tell you I have never been the same.

Kathy Shook Taylor is a first time author with her messages in I Love to Tell the Story of Jesus and His Love. She is currently employed by a Cancer Center in Spartanburg, South Carolina and has worked for the same physicians for over 32 very happy years. The idea of publishing was born out of a morning e-mail devotion sent out to her beloved co-workers and friends. These devotions were so well received, and with a growing e-mail audience, she was urged to publish these stories as a book of her pure devotion to God… Her goal? If there is any glory, if there is any praise, let it rise to God and that you, the reader, will *never again* wonder if you are loved.

TABLE OF CONTENTS

PREFACE

Dear Reader,

It is my pleasure to introduce to you a book that was inspired and encouraged by precious friends and coworkers as recipients of my morning e-mail devotionals. They have enlarged my territory by forwarding to their own personal covey of friends and family. I love and appreciate them so for their prayers on my behalf. Forever friends. What a treasure is mine!

It is my prayer that you, the reader, will find these writings uplifting and that they would remind you of just how much you are loved by your Creator.

HE CALLED ME DAUGHTER!

Jesus said unto her, "Daughter, you took a risk
of faith and now you are healed and whole. Live
well, live blessed, be healed of your plague."

Mark 5:34 (The Message)

I would like to tell my version of this story, in first
person, of a woman in Jesus's day who had an illness
described as an "issue of blood."

I must tell you that I am no better, but I feel that
I am growing worse day by day. I have had this issue
of blood now for twelve long years. I have spent all
of the money I have been through with doctor after
doctor. No one can help me. And this is no fault of
my own. I am so weak and so tired, and I am so alone
and desperately lonely. My husband will not even touch
me for I am ceremonially unclean. I am ostracized by
my temple friends. I am not even allowed to attend
the temple in this dreadful condition, and how I have
missed it for all of these years and have so missed the
fellowship I once had. But I have heard of a man called
Jesus and the wonderful things that he can do. I must
get to this Healer. He is my last hope.

Oh, the streets are so crowded with his many
followers! Could I quietly slip through this massive
throng of people to get just a little closer to Him? Oh,
I think I see Him. That must be him. Oh, yes. I see He
is walking up ahead! If I could just get close enough

to Him…if I could just get close enough to touch the hem of His garment, I know that I would be healed! I will silently slip just a little closer, stretch…reach out and touch with just my fingertip. There, I did it. Wait, Oh, hallelujah! Something just happened. I knew it. I just knew it! I am healed! I know it! I can feel it in my body. Oh, thank you! Thank you, God! I am healed! Oh, glory to God! For I am healed.

Jesus turned around, and he is looking in my direction. How could he know it was me? He is asking a question: "Who touched me?" His disciple said to him, "Master, you see all of these people pressed together and you ask who touched you?" But I heard Jesus reply to him, "I felt the power in my body go out from me."

I must go to him and tell him the whole truth. I will fall at his feet and simply tell him the whole truth. I am afraid and I am trembling, but I will go for he is asking.

"It was because of me, Master! I have been sick for so long and I have no money left…the doctors could not help me and I have only grown worse. It is widely known of your loving kindness and power. I just knew that if I could but touch the hem of your garment, I would be made whole. So I pressed through the crowds and I simply touched the hem of your robe, and thank you, my Master, for now I am healed, Jesus. Just as I knew I would be."

And do you know what the first word he said to me was, this Jewish Healer? Daughter!

Yes, that's right! Yes, he called me daughter! My friends told me that he might reprimand me as I was ceremonially unclean, but a reprimand? No indeed.

What I received from Jesus was compassion and tenderness and praise Him, healing! At long last! He said it was my faith that made me whole. And He called me daughter.

> Blessed Jesus, thank You for our beloved Scripture that tells us so much about You. Compassion, graciousness, tenderness, forgiveness, Your healing touch and the oh, so precious fact that You love us so very much. We will love and praise You forevermore.
>
> Thank you, Father, from Your daughters.

SERVING THE MASTER

Servants, do what you're told by your earthly masters. And don't just do the minimum that will get you by. Do your best. Work from the heart for your real Master, God, confident that you'll get paid in full when you come into your inheritance. Keep in mind always that the ultimate Master you're serving is Christ. The sullen servant who does shoddy work will be held responsible. Being a follower of Jesus doesn't cover up bad work.

Colossians 3:23–25 (The Message (MSG))

I just love the way Eugene Peterson interprets this beautiful verse in his translation "The Message." How applicable is this statement yet today, but having been written so very long ago. That is why the Bible is called the Living Word for God's Word is never outdated and applies to all stages of our lives.

In God's point of view, it matters not whether we are owners of the company or sweepers of the street, whatever our hand is given to do, we are to do it with all our might, heartily because, ultimately, God is our Boss and we are to strive to please him if we claim his name.

I believe that it is no accident that we are where we are in this very workplace today. I feel that he placed us here for a specific time and purpose. We all have bad days now and then, but our attitude can make or break our day. Do we wake up and say, "Good morning, Lord," or "Good Lord, it's morning"?

> Father God, thank you so much that we have somewhere to go in the mornings when so many do not. Many cannot find work. Many are not able to work. May we, from our hearts, appreciate this work that you have given our hands to do. May we approach our work with an attitude that pleases You. Thank you for the camaraderie that we share with each other and the feeling of family closeness that we also share. Please allow us greater compassion and kindness toward the patients that come to us for help.
>
> And, Father, would you continue to bless the employees of this office and its growth so that in serving others well, we will well serve you?
>
> In the lovely name of Christ,
> Amen

WHAT GOD WANTS

I don't find fault with your acts of worship, the frequent burnt sacrifices you offer, but why should I want your blue ribbon bull or more and more goats from your herds?

Psalm 50:8–9 (The Message)

For every beast of the forest is Mine and the cattle on a thousand hills.

Psalm 50:10 (King James Version)

Spread for Me a banquet of praise. Serve High God a feast of kept promises.

Psalm 50:14 (The Message)

Psalm 50:10 is a short verse that I committed to memory years ago because I thought it poetic and beautiful. But when I decided to use it in this devotion, I began to research a little bit and discovered so much meaning behind it.

The above scriptures are spoken by God to his beloved Israel. Outwardly, God's people were faithfully bringing their sacrifices before him as instructed, but inwardly, they had "lost their First Love" in that they had begun bringing their sacrifices to the altar out of habit. It had become routine and ritualistic to them. What was the use of going through the motions when their hearts were no longer in it, no praise or appreciation for the One that provided the sacrifice in the first place. Isn't that ironic? I just noticed this. He provided the sacrifices for them to sacrifice and then provided the Ultimate Sacrifice for us out of his heart of love. Thank you, my Father.

Suppose your own child gave you a Mother's Day gift or a Father's Day gift, but you knew there was no love or appreciation behind it. It was merely given because they felt it was their duty to show up with something. How would that make you feel?

That is what was happening with the Israelites. God didn't find fault with the sacrifices, but their motive and attitude was lacking. They were missing the point that God was their Loving Provider. There was no fellowship. No thankfulness. No devotion. God reminded them that he owned it all from the beginning; he didn't really need their bulls and goats. What he wanted was their devoted hearts, a desire to honor him, and their worshipful love.

So the next time you sit down to a warm loaf of bread and soft butter, please remember to thank Him for it. When you give your tithes and offerings, be thankful that you have it to give. Ask God to bless it and multiply it for His glory. Be thankful to Him that he gave you the strength and health to work it out and that you are healthy enough to be at church and toss it in the collection plate. God so loves a cheerful giver. Remember, too, the next time you drive or ride by a mossy green pasture dotted with wooly white lambs or brown baby calves, that our Lord God owns it all.

For which I am ever grateful.

Back of the bread is the snowy flour
And back of the flour is the mill
And back of the mill are the wheat, rain and sun
And the Holy Father's Will.

Maltbie D. Babcock
1858–1901

Praise you, dearest Father God, for all the gifts of goodness that we so often overlook. You are our loving Lord and Provider. We want to give you what you deserve and desire. We will love and honor you now and throughout eternity.

HE'S ASLEEP IN THE BOTTOM OF THE BOAT

And He was in the hinder part of the ship, asleep on a pillow: and they awake Him, and say unto Him, Master, carest thou not that we perish? And He arose, and rebuked the wind, and said unto the sea, Peace, be still. And the wind ceased, and there was a great calm.

Mark 4:38–40 (KJV)

The Book of Mark relays the story of Christ and his disciples getting into a boat to "pass over to the other side." Christ must have been weary and tired because He went to the stern of the ship, lay down, and drifted off to sleep. In the meantime, there arose a great storm with high winds and waves beating into the ship, so that now, it was taking on water. The disciples began to panic and go after Christ to wake him up and say, "Master, don't you care that we are perishing?"

So Christ rose up, rebuked the wind, and spoke to the sea, commanding it to be still, and Scripture says that there was a great calm. Praise your name, Father.

Can you just imagine being on that ship, so afraid for your very life with the wind howling about you and the waves crashing over the sides of the boat. That old wooden ship was probably creaking in the storm, furiously rocking to and fro tossed about by those relentless winds and turbulent waters. You fear you are near the end, but then…

Here comes the Sea Walker, the blind-man Healer, the leper-cleansing Man from Galilee! What blessed relief, oh, it's the Master of the Sea! All he had to do was speak, "Peace, be still." The winds cease, the waves stop, and the water became as smooth as glass. Not only has the storm calmed, but it calmed his disciples. Think of their relief and their marveling at this just-in-time miracle. How could they have had so little faith? Their Lord and Master was with them. He was just asleep in the bottom of the boat. All they had to do was to call on him. He came to their rescue. They said to one another, "What manner of man is this, that even the wind and the sea obey him?" Blessed Jesus!

A dear friend of mine, who I have known and loved for years, and I used to comfort one another with this story and say to each other, "It will be okay, remember, he is asleep in the bottom of the boat," when we would speak about the various storms in our lives. I found that so very comforting and still do.

God can speak peace to the storms in our lives or he may choose to quiet us with peace until the storm is over. Either way, my friend, don't be afraid. He is oh so near. Just call on him.

Oh, Glorious Comforter!

Just remember, he's asleep in the bottom of the boat.

GRACE? IT'S AMAZING!

Christ's Parable of the Vineyard Workers.

Matthew 20:1-16

For years, I struggled with the meaning of this puzzling parable of Christ's. Please take a minute or two and read this for yourself tonight. The following is my own paraphrase.

An employer goes out very early in the morning to hire workers for his vineyard. They agree upon the wage of a dollar for a day's work. So the hired hands get to work. Then about nine o'clock, the employer sees other men hanging around the town square without work. Employer tells them to get to work for a fair wage, so they go to work. The same thing happens at three o'clock and then again at the late hour of five o'clock. The employer finds more men having stood around all day and asks them, "Why are you standing around doing nothing?" They reply, "Because no one hired us." The employer says, "You can work in my vineyard."

When work day is finished, the employer tells foreman to call workers together and pay them their wages starting with the last hired and then going on to the first. Those hired at five o'clock were given a dollar, a day's wage. When those hired first saw this, they assumed that they would get more for having worked all day. But each man received a dollar. Taking it, they complained angrily that this was unfair, stating that the late workers worked one easy hour, and they were being made them equal to them having slaved all day under a scorching sun. Then employer says to the spokesman for the workers, "Friend, I have not been unfair to you. We agreed on the wage of a dollar, didn't we? I decided to give the last ones who came the same as you. Can't I do what I want with my own money? Are you going to be selfish because I am so generous?"

For years, I sided with the angry workers, trying to make sense of it. Why, this was totally unfair! It just made no sense. It simply was not fair compensation! Those late workers did not deserve the same wage as those that had worked all day long. Whatever was wrong with that employer? Didn't he get it? But it was me that didn't get it. Like me, do you ever get in your own way?

Then I read a most wonderful book by Phillip Yancey titled *What's So Amazing about Grace*? I had a light bulb moment. It was as clear as day now. I was right all along! Those late workers didn't deserve it! *Kathy*, that is the whole beautiful wonderful point! They did not deserve it. They were recipients of God's matchless grace! This was a parable about marvelous grace, an underserved gift from a loving, merciful, and forgiving God. God's riches at Christ's expense! Grace, grace, God's grace!

> Praise you, Father! Thank you that while we were yet sinners and so unlovely and so undeserving, Your sinless Son, Jesus the Christ, died for us. Glory to the Lamb!

WHEN GOD RAN

———

> So he got up and went to his father, but while
> the son was still a long way off, his father saw
> him and was filled with compassion. He ran,
> threw his arms around his neck and kissed him.
>
> Luke 15:20 (HCSB)

Christ tells the parable of the prodigal son in Luke's
Gospel. The word *prodigal*, used as an adjective
in this verse, means "living recklessly or being
wastefully extravagant."

This is my paraphrase of the story. There was a
man with two sons. The younger one said to his father,
"Father, give me my share of your estate." So the father
divided the property between the sons and the young
son gathered his belongings and left the home that
he knew so well. A distant land, a faraway place was
"calling" him. In this foreign land, he squandered his
wealth in wild living. After he had spent everything,
there was a severe famine in the whole country and he
began to be in need. So he went and hired himself out
to a citizen of that country who sent him to his fields
to feed his pigs.

According to the law of Moses, pigs were considered
to be unclean animals. They were not to be used for
food nor were they to be used in sacrifice, and here he
sits, this young Jewish boy among the pigs. To even
touch the food that the pigs ate was considered unclean.

Scripture relates that he became so hungry (remember he had spent all—he had nothing left) that he longed to fill his belly with the pigs' food. As a Jewish boy, he had sunk to his lowest. But then, Scripture says that he came to his senses. (Don't you just love that?) He realized the state he was in. He said to himself, "How many of my father's hired servants have food to spare, and here I am, starving to death. I will go back to my father and say to him, 'Father, I have sinned against heaven and against you and am no longer worthy to be called your son, make me as one of your hired servants.'"

So he got up and turned around to go back home. This, my friend, is Repentance 101, which is what it takes. You realize the state you are in and you turn away from your sin and go to the Father, confessing.

I love imagining this next scene. The son is on his way home, starving, worn out, and probably smelling like the pigs that he had been working with. Can't you see just him on the long dusty road home, alone? Probably with long labored steps and stooped shoulders with overwhelming feelings of guilt and shame, wondering if his father would accept him as one of the hired servants or not. What he does not know is that he is in for a loving and forgiving surprise.

And here is Daddy, pacing the floor from window to door, no doubt many times a day, looking for his lost boy. "Oh, where is my son? How I miss him. How I love him…I am so worried about him. Is he hungry? Is he in want? I wish he would come home where he could have what he needs, where I could love him and take care of him again." So he goes to the door one more time. Scripture says that the father saw the son "while he was still a great way off"!

The father *ran* to his son and the King James Version reads that "he fell on his son's neck" (I love that too!), threw his arms around him, and kissed him, joyfully, happily welcoming his son home.

My friends, this is a beautiful depiction of God running to the repentant sinner who is on his way back to Him. Running to me. Running to you. Dear one, if you have not given your heart and life to Christ, please do not wait any longer. You simply don't know what you are missing. Ask God from a repentant heart to forgive your sin; ask him to come into your heart and life. Tell him that you want to come home.

If you do, you will never be the same. If you do, he will *run* to you.

A BEARER OF GOOD NEWS

How lovely on the mountain are the feet of
those who bring good news, who proclaim
peace, who bring good tidings, who proclaim
salvation, who say to Zion, "Our God Reigns!"

Isaiah 52:7

Greetings and welcome in the lovely name of
Jesus. He is the Rose of Sharon, the Lily of the
Valley, the Bright and Morning Star! He is the
altogether Lovely One!

This was a salutation given often by my childhood
pastor, the Reverend Donald Seay, to the congregation
before his sermon at the Arcadia Free Will Baptist
Church. Preacher Seay was full of the joy of the Lord.
He could simply make scripture come alive. He shouted
his praise often, loud, and long and sometimes with
infectious booming laughter. He was a young but old-
fashioned preacher who was not afraid to preach hell—
hot—and heaven, oh so sweet. He loved the Lord so
much. You could see it in his smiling eyes. He enjoyed
the music so in our church, and my, what a beautiful
singing voice he had! One of his often requested songs
was my cherished and spellbinding "The Stranger of
Galilee." My sister would accompany him on the organ.
There was, to me, a holy hush all over the sanctuary
as he sang this reverent song about his Christ. There
was hardly a dry eye in the place. It is difficult to even

remember it without a few joyful tears. Allow me, please, just a recollection of a few lovely lyrics.

> In fancy I stood by the shore one day of the beautiful murmuring sea. I saw the great crowds as they thronged the way of the Stranger of Galilee. My shackles fell off at His pierced Feet. Oh, my friend, won't you love him forever, so gracious and tender is He. Proclaim Him today as your Savior, this Stranger of Galilee.

Donnie Seay was a dear friend and pastor to the extended Shook family for many years, visiting when we were sick, coming to anoint us with oil as the Scripture instructs, or just coming by in the evenings for sweet fellowship, and he never left us without a prayer offered on our behalf and prayed for each one of us by name. How I miss his genuine heartfelt prayers and hearing his familiar knock on our door.

Preacher Seay has now gone home to his beloved Christ. In my immaturity of youth, I didn't tell him how much I appreciated him, how much I loved him, and how much I feel he taught me. But I will get another chance one day and how I look forward to that when I know that he will say to me in his booming voice:

> Greetings and welcome, Kathy, in the lovely name of Jesus! He is the Rose of Sharon, the Lily of the Valley, the Bright and Morning Star! For he is the altogether Lovely One!

And then we will shout and rejoice together while the ages roll on.

If there is a bearer of good news in your life, a minister, a Sunday school teacher, a friend, don't wait too late to tell them how much they mean to you, how much you appreciate them, and how much they have taught you. Tell them you are praying for them.

Do it now, so they will be encouraged and inspired to keep on keeping on, bearing the Good News, which will be wonderful for us all.

AND WHO IS HE TO YOU?

He saith unto them, "But whom say ye that I am?" And Simon Peter answered and said, "Thou art the Christ, the Son of the living God." And Jesus answered and said unto him, "Blessed art thou, Simon Bar-jona: for flesh and blood hath not revealed it unto thee, but my Father which is in heaven."

Matthew 16:15–17 (KJV)

Jesus was widely recognized as a great man throughout all of Israel. But sadly, the most of them did not understand who he really was. On Christ's inquiry of the disciples as to who the people were saying that he was, they told Jesus that some were calling him John the Baptist and some said of him that he was a prophet. But then, Jesus posed the same question to his own disciples who had spent so much time with him, observing his miracles, breaking bread with him, traveling about with him, and listening to his profound teachings. Peter, one of Christ's disciples, got it. He spoke up out of the twelve and declared to Jesus that he was the Christ, the Son of the living God. And Jesus blessed him.

Peter did not learn this wonderful fact from the world around him. Mortal man did not inform Peter of Christ's deity, but our Father God revealed this truth to Peter. It is so important to God that we understand just who Christ is. He *is* who he claimed to be. We can rest in that. He can be trusted. He proved himself to be our Savior, conquering death, hell, and the grave. He is the Risen Savior, alive forevermore. He is our heaven connection. He is our God connection. We cannot make heaven our home without Jesus. We cannot know the One True God without Jesus.

You and I have heard people in this very day and age offering this very same worldly opinion that was given over 2,000 years ago: that Jesus was a great teacher or a great prophet.

It is crucial that we make our own personal decision as to who Jesus was and is, not by listening to others or going with the crowd's opinion, whether right or wrong. We, as individuals, must confess that Jesus is the Son of the living God.

Prayerfully consider this critical, most important question. Examine for yourself, "Who do you say that he is?"

FIFTY SHADES OF GREEN

God spoke: "Earth, green up! Grow all varieties of seed-bearing plants, every sort of fruit-bearing tree." And there it was. Earth produced green seed-bearing plants, all varieties, and fruit-bearing trees of all sorts. God saw that it was good. It was evening, it was morning—Day Three.

Genesis 1:11–13 (The Message)

When I was searching for Scripture for this reflection, I was so tickled to see that The Message described Day Three of Creation in this manner, I had to laugh. Seems I could just see and hear God snapping his holy fingers and commanding the earth with his one-of-a-kind voice to "Green up, Earth!" And the earth obeyed, and God blessed it when he saw that it was good. What a mighty God we serve that even the earth obeys him.

This year, for some reason, I have fallen in love with April. I was out early Saturday morning and began to notice how many different shades of green that this spring month has to offer. Our pretty section of the earth is coming back to life, a reminder of the blessed resurrection. The ground is beginning to warm, which makes the sap rise in the trees, which, in turn, ushers out those tender and oh-so-pale green leaves on those dark brown branches with a soft apple green. What a lovely combination. Then I began to notice all these shades of emerald, jade, chartreuse, green with a hint of red, soft green, and milky white. Not to mention the ever faithful rich dark evergreen. Green is my favorite color, and it happens to be the first color mentioned in the Scriptures. God must love it too as there is so much of it: rolling green hills, deep green forests, frothy pale green and white hydrangeas, sturdy green stems for those heady yellow daffodils, softest green pastures.

Many of my friends have heard me say, I'm sure, that I am so thankful that our God loves variety, color, and texture. The Master Artist could have made everything the same color or really no color at all—we wouldn't have known the difference, but I believe that he loves us so much that he wants us to enjoy even the smallest and most intricate detail of his world. He created it all for us to enjoy. He wants us to simply marvel at his Creation, and the older I get, the more I do.

I have enjoyed so many springs by now, but at this one, I feel that during an unusually quiet moment for me, God softly reminded me to pay special attention to my beautiful surroundings and the gifts that He has provided for my enjoyment. You see, He knows how I love green.

April will soon be over. Early one morning, would you take just a moment to walk outside alone, quiet yourself, and be still? The air is so sweet in an early cool April morning. Take time to notice it, and in that blessed stillness, note the beauty that surrounds you. He created this April love for you.

Tell him that you love Him for it. Tell Him that you appreciate all those wonderfully unique shades of green. Tell Him that you just love the artist in Him. It will simply make His day…and yours.

FAN THE FLAME!

———

You are going to find out that there will be times when people will have no stomach for solid teaching, but will fill up on spiritual junk food—catchy opinions that tickle their fancy. They'll turn their backs on truth and chase mirages. But you—keep your eye on what you're doing; accept the hard times along with the good; Keep the Message Alive; do a thorough job as God's servant."

2 Timothy 4:3–5 (The Message)

The above scripture is taken from Paul's letter to Timothy. Paul, the apostle, was a Christian missionary taking the Gospel of Christ to the first century world. His passion was Christ and he was one of the most influential Christians of all time and wrote a great portion of the New Testament. At the time of this writing to Timothy, Paul was in a Roman prison for preaching the Gospel. Paul knew that he was near the end of his life. He was passing the torch to Timothy, a younger believer who had traveled with Paul on his missionary journeys, exhorting him to keep the message alive, fan the flame, pass it on.

My Bible fellowship class has been studying 2 Timothy, and it is fascinating. I have the blessing of not just one teacher, but three of the finest teachers around. They make you want to come up higher. Interestingly, this past Sunday morning, as I was dressing for church,

I was listening to a well-known host who had three guests on her program billed as the new up-and-coming spiritual advisers. I stopped briefly to take a look at them. They were beautiful young people. Educated, clean-cut, socially aware. The three of them were touted as being savvy, having developed self-made businesses, writing reflective best sellers, and were on the lecturing circuit to sold-out crowds with advice about how to enrich your lives. I thought, to myself, how ironic that we are in the middle of this study of 2 Timothy, which warned about this very subject. I began to think about the young people in the sold-out crowds. They are searching for something to enrich their lives. They are listening to these three beautiful people. Because what's not to like? It sounds good on the surface because the majority of what they say has an element of truth in it. They say give to others, not what can I get but what can I give? Be aware and grateful to God for everything as it will change the way that you feel on the inside. They say they see God in everything, even in a fuzzy puppy. They say forgiveness is key and that you must forgive others.

What could possibly be wrong with those positive thoughts?

But please notice that not one mention of Jesus the Christ is made. They mention God, which sounds good. A warm fuzzy feeling, right? But you cannot have the true God of the Bible without Christ. Because it is the Son of God who leads us to God. It is Christ who teaches us to give to others with no thought of ourselves. It is Christ who teaches us to thank God in all things.

It is Christ who teaches us that God is his Father and ours. It is Christ who taught us that forgiveness is key as he so lovingly and willingly demonstrated at Calvary.

Beloved, you simply cannot leave Christ out of the equation. That is what the deceiver would have us believe. Satan is the great imitator. He wants our young people to believe that you can have an enriched life without Christ. He wants to fill them up on spiritual junk food, a warm fuzzy feeling, and tickle their ears with half-truths. He has been the deceiver since the day of Adam. Don't let him have our young! Your children, your precious grandchildren, your nieces, your nephews. Teach them, I implore you, that Christ is our model for an enriched heaven-bound and forgiven life. A profound quote from one of my teachers— used with permission: "The Gospel of Jesus Christ is just one generation from extinction at all times. It is the responsibility of all who know Jesus to pass that knowledge on to others."

So fan the flame of Jesus Christ! Pass the torch of Jesus the Christ! Pass on the precious life-giving message of Jesus the Christ! Exhort your own Timothy as Paul did, and please don't let the message die with you.

I WANT TO BE AN ONESIPHORUS!

> May the Lord show mercy to the household
> of Onesiphorus because he often refreshed me
> and was not ashamed of my chains.
>
> 2 Timothy 1:16 (NIV)

What a name! Onesiphorus. This unusual name means "Profit Bearer" and is pronounced *Oh-ne h-see-fuh-ruhs*. Sounds like a sneeze, doesn't it? It belongs to a dear friend of Paul's and is forever recorded in Scripture history not once, but twice. Paul remembers him fondly in his second letter to Timothy.

These are the last days of Paul's life, being a Roman prisoner, in chains for preaching the good news of Christ. He is an old man at this point and is near death. He is recalling that many of his friends had deserted him, but this friend stayed true to Paul and it was Onesiphorus. Scripture tells us that he went to Rome, seeking Paul out, and visited him in prison. He was not ashamed to be known as a comrade to this great man of God. Paul also reminds Timothy, "You know very well in how many ways he helped me in Ephesus."

Paul, of course, had the presence of the Lord to encourage his spirit while in that dark, dank, cold Roman dungeon used as a prison. But God used Onesiphorus to encourage Paul in the flesh. God inspired Paul to write about him so that we could benefit from knowing about him and to be challenged by his good character and selfless giving. I imagine it was probably a bit dangerous to be a friend to Paul during those days as he was the leader of the Christian movement. So Onesiphorus must have been a courageous man. Nothing specific is mentioned about the ways in which Onesiphorus encouraged Paul, but just the mere act of coming to visit him, seeking him out, and remembering him in his hour of need would have probably been enough for Paul. Simply to be remembered is oh so wonderful.

Is there someone in your life today that needs to be remembered? Any simple act of kindness may seem insignificant to you, but if you are the one in need, it is a welcome breath of fresh air. A cool drink of water is enjoyed most by the one who is thirsting. Ask God to bring to mind someone that needs remembering today. Someone that needs to share a burden. He will surely do it. He may just need to use an Onesiphorus in someone's life today.

Would you allow him to use you?

> Father, thank you for the example of Onesiphorus. Thank you that he befriended and encouraged our dear Paul in that Roman prison. Allow us, too, to be useful in your kingdom, just as was Onesiphorus. May we honor you today in lightening someone's load, sharing someone's burden, and following your precious lead.
>
> In the name of our Burden Bearer, Jesus the Christ. Amen.

STAY CLOSE TO YOUR SHEPHERD

All we like sheep have gone astray, we have
turned everyone to his own way.

Isaiah 53:6 (KJV)

Have you an old church hymn that you love? Gosh,
I have so many. I miss them a great deal now as our
modern-day churches don't sing them as they once did.
One of my favorites was written by Robert Robinson
at the age of twenty-three in 1758, "Come Thou Fount
of Every Blessing."

O to grace how great a debtor/ Daily I'm
constrained to be / Let thy goodness, like
a fetter / Bind my wandering heart to thee /
Prone to wander, Lord I feel it, Prone to leave
the God I love / Here's my heart, Lord take and
seal it / Seal it for thy courts above.

I thought this song fitting with the Scripture chosen
above. The Bible oftentimes refers to Jesus's followers
as sheep with Jesus being our Loving Shepherd.
Interesting fact about sheep—they are prone to wander,
too, without their shepherd leading them. They can get
into dangerous trouble and quickly if they wander away
from the flock and their shepherd. If they strike out
on their own path, they are more vulnerable to their
natural predators and sheep cannot defend themselves.
Sometimes, the shepherd will have to go out and find

the lost sheep and bring it back into the safety of the fold. So it is with us.

I know that in my own Christian life, I am more vulnerable to my predator, the deceiver, if I begin to drift too far away from Christ for whatever reason. If I become discouraged, if I don't stay in the Word like I should, if I don't fellowship with other believers enough, if I let unforgiveness creep slowly into my life, even if I don't get enough rest and am super tired. I am easy prey. I must stay close to my Shepherd.

In John, chapter 8, Satan is called the father of lies, and it is his primary aim to lead us astray, away from our Shepherd. Satan wants to separate us from God.

> 1 Peter 5:8 in the New American Standard Bible (NASB) reads: "Be of sober spirit, be on the alert. *Your adversary, the devil, prowls around like a roaring lion seeking someone to devour.*"

This God-inspired Scripture was written for our protection.

Make no mistake, my friend.

Satan does not play, so we simply must be on guard.

You don't want to face the roaring lion alone in your own lives, so…stay close to your Shepherd.

HE WASHED THE FEET
OF HIS BETRAYER

After that he poureth water into a basin, and
began to wash the disciples' feet, and to wipe
them with the towel wherewith He was girded.

John 13:5 (KJV)

During the time of Christ, if you were a guest at dinner,
it was the custom for you to have your feet washed at
the door as you had probably traveled all day on dusty
roads with sandaled feet. This menial task was usually
assigned to the lowest of the servants.

For Christ and his disciples, the Last Supper took
place in an upper room. On this particular night, there
was no servant to perform the washing of Christ's and
the disciples' feet. It never occurred to the disciples
to take it upon themselves to wash the feet of their
companions, not to mention their Lord and Master.

But it was their own precious Master Jesus in an
awesome act of humility on that lonely night, taking
off his outer garment, wrapping a towel about Himself,
pouring a basin of fresh clean water, kneeling down and
began to wash the dusty feet of his disciples.

I love imagining this scene. Picture your own self as
one of his disciples (you are, you know).

So here he is, the King of Kings, the Lord of Glory,
the Everlasting Father kneeling down in front of you in

a pure act of great love and humility to wash the very dust off of your dirty feet with hands that formed you from the dust of the ground, with hands that set the sun, moon, and stars in place. With holy sinless hands that would soon be pierced with nails to a rugged cross for you.

My dear Jesus washed even the feet of his betrayer that night, knowing full well what Judas was about to do.

> For He knew Him who would betray Him, therefore He said, "You are not all clean."
>
> John 13:11

Yet Christ was servant to them every one, loving them all, dying for them all. Even Judas.

> Holy Father—what manner of love? That Jesus could stoop down in humility and love and wash his betrayer's feet, knowing what was in the heart of Judas and what was about to happen is a deep mystery. Mere mortal man in the flesh could not do this, Father. Only You, My God.

THOMAS, THE DOUBTER

———

Then saith He to Thomas, Reach hither they
finger, and behold my hands; and reach hither
thy hand, and thrust it into my side: and be not
faithless, but believing.

John 20:27 (KJV)

The Gospel of John tells of an appearance of Christ
after he was resurrected from the dead. It describes
the disciples being assembled together in a room, for
fear of the Jews. The doors were shut, and Jesus came
and stood in their midst and said unto them, "Peace be
unto you."

Those words, "the doors were shut," just thrill me.
There the band of followers were, huddled in that
room, fearfully talking about the recent events of the
arrest, trial, and crucifixion of their Lord and Master,
with the door closed, and suddenly, there stands Jesus
in front of them! Can you picture it! Jesus was right
there with them, speaking peace to them. He showed
them his hands and his side. Scripture goes on to say
that the disciples were glad when they saw the Lord.
That must have been some more reunion.

For some unexplained reason, one of the disciples,
Thomas, was not with them on this special night. But
when the disciples saw Thomas, I can just imagine how
excited they must have been to relay this fascinating
story to him. Something like this.

Man, Thomas! Brother, you really missed it!
We saw the Lord! Yes! Yes, we did! Oh, I wish
you could have been there! He just appeared,
Thomas, out of nowhere in the same room with
us! No, really, Thomas! Believe it, Thomas…
For it is truth. The doors were shut and all of a
sudden, He was right there with us!

But Thomas didn't buy it. He actually said to them:

Except I see the print of the nails in his hands
and touch His pierced side, I will not believe.

Doubting Thomas didn't know it then, but he was
about to get his chance.

Eight days later, the disciples were gathered together
again and Thomas was now with them. The door,
again, was shut, and Jesus appeared to them, again,
"Peace be unto you." And precious loving Jesus singled
Thomas out this time and said to him, "Reach hither
they finger, and behold my hands; and reach hither thy
hand and thrust it into my side: and be not faithless,
but believing."

And Thomas answered and said unto Jesus, "My
Lord and my God."

Did you notice how Jesus so gently responded to
Thomas's unbelief? He didn't ridicule him in front of
the others. He didn't say harshly, "I am ashamed of you
Thomas for not believing. Go ahead, have it your way.
Touch my scars. Now do you believe?"

No, no, no! I know that Christ would never do
that. Just listen in your heart to His gentle voice softly
bidding, "Be not faithless, Thomas, but believe."

I am not sure why Thomas was not with the others on that first night. But Jesus knows. Jesus knew exactly what Thomas would say when he was told by the other disciples that they had seen Him. I believe with all my heart that Christ came back especially for Thomas that night, to dispel his unbelief and doubt. To give him blessed hope.

> Jesus met Thomas at his point of need. I also believe that Christ will go to any length for us to help us believe. He did for Thomas. Why not for you and me?
>
> Listen closely. Is he whispering to you? Be not faithless, but believing.

WHY NOT SING TO HIM?

I will sing to the Lord as long as I live. I will
praise my God to my last breath.

Psalm 104:33 (NLT)

Have you ever sung a song to God? The psalmist
David did. He danced before the Lord, and he played
instruments unto the Lord. David was a happy, joyful
believer and took pleasure in his loving relationship
with God. And I believe that God accepted and loved
his exuberant praise that rose to the very heavens.

Even though David being human, as we are, had
sin in his own life and suffered because of it, he was
committed to God. God said of David that he is "a man
after my own heart."

How I would love to think that very God would
say of me, that I was a "woman after His own heart."
How thrilling and humbling that would be. Wouldn't
you like that said of you too?

Israel's King David wrote many of the Psalms, one
of my favorite books of the Bible. Full of praise and
adoration of God, the Father. Do yourself a favor and
spend some quality time in this book, it will, without
a doubt, bless you. The Psalms were hymns, if you
will, that were used in Jewish and Christian worship.
They are simply beautifully written with the most
picturesque language one can imagine. Like this one
in Psalm 42.

As the deer pants for the water so my soul longs
after thee. You alone are my heart's desire and I
long to worship thee. [my paraphrase]

How could you not love that? Simple eloquent poetry!

At your next quiet time, when you are alone with
God, why not start off with a heartfelt song of praise
to him? Focus on his goodness to you and your family
with thanksgiving. It will still, clear, and ready your
mind in preparation for your devotional time with him
in his Word.

It matters not to him if you have a "voice." Only if
you have a song in your heart because of him. You are
alone with him, praising your God, and your praise will
rise to the very heavens, as David's did, as an offering,
a sweet melodic sound to his ears. His beloved child,
singing praises unto him. I have it on good authority
that He will simply love this sacrificial act. I believe He
will bless you for it and He will draw close to you as his
Word promises, when you draw close to Him.

Don't be afraid and don't be shy about it. Let it spring
from your sincere heart and just make a joyful noise.

It might just be a quiet time you will never forget.

HOW GOD SPEAKS TODAY

> God, who at various times and in various
> ways spoke in times past to the fathers by the
> prophets, has in these last days spoken to us by
> His Son, whom He has appointed heir of all
> things.
>
> Hebrews 1:1–2

This week, I read what was a very disturbing story to me. The story was of a woman, her two children, and her own mother walking down a public street naked. All of them, not just one of them, all four of them, naked, without benefit of even a shoe, walking down a public street. This was traumatic and sad enough, but the saddest thing to me was the answer they gave when questioned by the police and their reason for doing it. They told police that "the Lord told us to do this."

Believers in Jesus the Christ know full well that God speaks to us through the Scripture in current day. He speaks through his Word to us and through the Holy Spirit sent to us by Jesus who lives within us when we are true believers in Christ. Beloved, if you receive "a word" that you believe is from Almighty God, and it does not line up with the God-inspired holy Word in the Scriptures, then it is not God speaking to your heart.

This display was disturbing to me because nonbelievers laugh at such bizarre behavior and taunt the believing world with outlandish events such as this, throwing shadows on our witness of the Light of the World. I feel that these bizarre acts are an attempt of the deceiver to diminish our testimony, and he uses them to grow further doubt in the nonbelieving world and broaden its numbers.

God does not audibly speak today as he did in the days of Moses. Again, he speaks through his Word. If you want to know what plan God has for your life, then go to the Bible, pray, and find out. If you want to know how to have a closer relationship with him, go to your Bible and find out. If you want to know how to handle a conflict with your neighbor, go to your Bible. Scripture even informs us of how to dress. If you want to know what God wants you to do, go to your beloved Word of God. This beautiful and treasured gift from God has all of the answers we need for this earthly and soon-to-be heavenly life.

Please, believers, be ready with your answer to those who approach you with nonsensical stories such as this questioning our very faith and finally give praise, honor, and glory to our holy and perfect God.

A BOTTLE OF YOUR TEARS

Put thou my tears into thy bottle: are they not
in thy book?

Psalm 56:8 (KJV)

Did you know that according to the psalmist David,
God keeps our tears in a bottle and records them in his
book? God is well aware of our feelings, for what and
how we suffer, and he keeps accurate records.

I have read and believe that when you are at your
lowest point and sorrows abound on every hand that
that is when God is nearest to you. It may seem to us, at
this point, that God is the furthest away that he could
possibly be. You may find Him so distant and silent
that you wonder if He even knows what is going on
in your life, but rest assured that he does know and he
does care. The Bible tells us this truth. When we get
to this point in our lives, it is important for us to focus
on prayer and the Word, stay connected, lean into Him
when we need Him the most, even if we don't feel like
it. Talk to Him, even if you don't feel like it. This is
when we are to walk by faith and not by sight as the
Scripture instructs us. And He will reward our faith.

Isaiah, the prophet, prophesied that the coming
Messiah would be "a man of sorrows acquainted with
grief." Do you remember in Scripture when Jesus cried?
He cried at the tomb of Lazarus, knowing that he was
going to bring him back to life, but he loved Lazarus,

having been a guest in his home and had broken bread with him on many occasions, yet Jesus cried at his death. Lazarus was his close friend.

Another recorded event of Christ crying was during his triumphal entry of Jerusalem, before his crucifixion, riding on a donkey colt. Scripture says that when he approached the city and saw Jerusalem, He wept over it. His beloved chosen people who rejected him as being their long awaited Holy One.

Yes, Christ knows what sorrow feels like. He knows what deep despair feels like. He knows what lonely rejection of a people he loves so dearly feels like. And he is acquainted with our sorrow. He can relate. Because He has been there and done that and He knows how you feel.

But one glad day, God can store that precious bottle of tears on a high shelf because in our new heavenly home, the Book of Revelation tells us that God Himself will wipe away every tear; there will be no more death, no more mourning, no more gravesides, no crying or pain for the first things have passed away. Hallelujah to the Precious Lamb of God for there will be Joy in his Holy Presence forevermore.

Yes, weeping may endure for a night, but joy comes in the morning.

APPLES OF GOLD

A Word fitly spoken is like apples of gold in pictures of silver.

Proverbs 25:11 (KJV)

King Solomon wrote these lovely picturesque words above to describe the right word spoken at the right time. Solomon was the son of David, king of Israel. When Solomon succeeded his father as king, he asked the Lord for a discerning heart and wisdom to rule his people. And God was so pleased and honored that he granted Solomon's request. Solomon is said to have been the wisest man to ever live then, and there would be none wiser than him in the future.

Have you ever had a friend that knew just what to say to you and just at the right time? Over my lifetime, I have been blessed with so many.

My beautiful sister, like a mother to me, could soothe the drama of my young years like no one else. When I read Proverbs 25:11, my sweet sister comes to my mind instantly. She was and is an, oh-so-generous giver of apples of gold.

In my early twenties, I was going through a particularly rough spot that lasted much longer than I would have wanted it to. But my dear friend, Emily, my sister in Christ, gave me many apples of gold. God must surely have whispered in her ear so often that Kathy needs a golden apple today, then I would get this oh-so-comforting card in the mail that was so fitting for the moment. I have saved them all. Comforting, assuring, "everything is going to be all right" cards. How did she know that I needed that on that day? It must have been God. It was always right on time. It is just like God to comfort in such a way. He is always right on time.

Do you know someone that needs encouragement today, maybe someone going through a dark time in their life? Trouble in their marriage, a problem on their job? Someone who might be going through a period of doubting their faith? Choose someone today and give them a golden apple, a word fitly spoken, to lift them up and inspire them to keep on keeping on. Send a card to someone who needs a kind word so badly. An out-of-the-blue phone call to someone that needs a cheerful voice. A treasure that they will never forget.

You know, Scripture tells us that we reap what we sow. It just might lift your spirit too!

> Father God, how grateful I am for you and to you for my enormous gleaming silvery basket full of beautiful golden apples, bursting at the seams and spilling over that I have received over my lifetime from family, friends, loved ones, you, and am still receiving. How gracious you are, my Lord, as you know just what we need and when we need it and you provide. How loving of you. Just to be able to remember and reflect on all received is yet another golden apple. You are so amazing.

Thank you for your inspired Word to Solomon so many years ago that inspires us still today.

In the name of my loving Jehovah Jireh (the Lord is my Provider, Genesis 22:14), Amen.

IS YOUR COMMUNICATION CORRUPT?

Let no corrupt communication proceed out of your mouth, but that which is good, to the use of edifying, that it may bring Grace unto the hearers.

Ephesians 4:29 (KJV)

Watch the way you talk. Let nothing foul or dirty come out of your mouth. Say only what helps, each word a gift.

Ephesians 4:29 (The Message)

Yet another centuries-old verse that is so applicable today, remembering that we call the Bible the Living Word. Scripture says that God's Word will never pass away. Heaven and earth will, but not his Living Word. You gotta love that!

To edify means to "build up, illuminate, enlighten, not tear down." God instructs us in the above verse to guard our mouths, being careful to encourage each other with our words and not tear down each other's confidence. You know that little silly rhyme we learned as children about sticks and stones can break my bones, but words will never hurt me? Lies. All lies. The part about the words not hurting is a bold-faced lie. Words are so, so hurtful and can make you ache and you can carry that ache throughout your adult life. Someone once said that you may not remember what I look like or what I say exactly, but you will always remember how I made you feel. That is a sobering thought.

I had a little grammar school friend who was always telling me she was prettier than me, smarter than me, had more friends than me, prettier clothes than me, which was all true by the way, but talk about bringing me down! The more she said, the worse I felt and the more I wanted her as a friend. Twisted, right? Fifty years later, that stuff is still hard to forget, even when spoken by a child. I am so over it now, but I still remember it.

Our mouths can get us into great trouble, can wreck family relationships. It can get us fired from our jobs. It can render you friendless. It can damage your children for a lifetime. It can crush someone's spirit to the bare bone. We simply must guard our tongues. Did you know that blessing and cursing can be uttered out of the same mouth? The Scripture says so. When you reflect on that truth, it is hard to imagine. How can that be?

My words to you should be as The Message relates. A lovely gift, beautifully wrapped, I should say only what helps you, encourages you and edifies you, so that I might bring grace to you, and do so with love in the Spirit of Jesus the Christ.

I am Master of my unspoken word

And slave to the ones that should have remained unspoken.

A SUNRISE BREAKFAST ON THE BEACH!

When they got out on land, they saw a charcoal
fire in place, with fish laid out on it and bread.

John 21:9 (ESV)

At the third appearance of Christ after the Resurrection,
at the seashore of Tiberius, he cooks breakfast for
the disciples!

Imagine this scene. On the horizon, a rosy sunrise
with puffy golden peach-colored clouds and breakfast
of sizzling, beautifully grilled fish and fresh hot bread
on a charcoal fire, on the beach prepared by none other
than Jesus the Christ. How awesome is that? Talk about
a way to start off your day! This is how it came about.

After the Resurrection, the disciples, Peter, Thomas,
Nathanael, the sons of Zebedee, and two others were
together one night. Peter says, "I'm going fishing." The
others said to him, "We'll go with you." You know,
most of them were fishermen by trade. It was probably
comforting to them to do something familiar after
all of the hurt and loss they had suffered through the
crucifixion of Christ and not having him with them
daily as they once had enjoyed. I am sure that they
missed him greatly.

Well, just as day was breaking, Jesus stood on the
shore, yet the disciples did not know that it was Jesus.

Jesus called out to them, "Children, do you have any fish?" They answered him, "No." Jesus said to them, "Cast the net on the right side of the boat, and you will find some."

So they cast out onto the right side of the boat, and now they could not haul it all in because of the great number of fish. 153 large fish! John said to Simon Peter, "It is the Lord!" They immediately recognized his miraculous work! Well, impetuous Peter dove right into the sea and hurriedly swam to shore. The others came up in the boat, dragging the net full of fish as they were not too far from land. When they came ashore, they saw and, no doubt, smelled the aroma of the delicious feast that Christ had prepared for them. He knew that they had been fishing all night, with not a catch, and would be tired and hungry. Jesus said to them, "Come and have breakfast!" And Jesus took bread and gave it to them and so with the fish.

Wasn't that tender and thoughtful of Jesus to prepare a meal for His disciples..? And He served them that beautiful morning with a cool sea breeze about them and the sweet rhythmic music of the water. I wish I could have been there to witness and capture that awesome moment in time. I feel certain that Christ missed his disciples too, having been with them every day for nearly three years. He loved them so much, had taught them much and He would soon pass the Torch onto them and they were to carry on His work in the Ministry. They, too, would pass the Torch on. Christ knew that He would soon have to leave them for a long while and I believe He wanted to spend just a little more time with them before He must go back to His Father.

Yes, even more evidence here that Christ loved his followers and longed to fellowship with them. Spending quality time with them, loving them, feeding them, body and soul, as He longs to do with us. Some Glorious Day to come, I believe we will hear Him call to us, "My Children, Come and dine with Me"! Then we will sit down together with Him and the disciples, Moses, David, Abraham, our precious loved ones, break bread together and just fellowship around the Table of Christ with joy and love. Oh! Won't it be wonderful there?

You know, I believe He looks forward to that day too.

THE GARMENT OF PRAISE MAKES ALL THE DIFFERENCE

> Put on the garment of praise for the spirit of heaviness.
>
> Isaiah 61:3

Now, wait a minute, you read that a little too fast. Please go back and read this Scripture again. It has a message in it just for you. Good, now. Isn't that a beautiful verse? And there is such truth in it. We are going to learn how to put this verse into action in our lives.

If you are like me, you have had times of loneliness, heavyheartedness, and just simply feeling down. Sometimes, you might not even be able to pinpoint the actual problem. King David, who wrote the majority of the poetic Psalms, started many of these writings in a downcast mood. For instance, Psalm 102. Read it carefully when you get a moment to see what I mean. See what a change came over him at the end of this writing.

To paraphrase a bit of it, David begins with "Hear my prayer, O Lord. And let my cry come to you. Do not hide your face from me in the day of my trouble. Incline your ear to me in the day that I call. Answer me speedily! (Don't we say this too? Hurry up, God, I need an answer—now!) My heart is stricken and withered like grass so that I forget to eat my bread. My drink is mingled with my weeping."

I would say that David was down, wouldn't you agree?

But then in verse 12, his heart begins to turn around because he began to put on that garment of praise that is described in the Book of Isaiah. He began to look up and remember the power of his Almighty God:

> Of old, You laid the foundation of the earth and the heavens are the work of your Hands. (He remembers God the Creator.) They will perish, but You will endure. Yes they will all grow old like a garment. Like a cloak you will change them (heaven and earth, God will change one glad day). But you are the same (David remembers that God is never-changing, he can trust him). Your years will have no end. The children of your servants will continue and their descendants will be established before You. (Parenthesis mine)

Quite a difference from one end of this Psalm to the other, wouldn't you say? The garment of praise made all the difference. David encouraged his own self and we can too! The next time you begin to feel down with doubt and fear begins to creep in to your heart, imagine yourself slipping into a lovely garment of praise. Really visualize it, with words of praise written on it as you wrap it securely and snuggly around you.

> My God never changes. He is the same yesterday, today, and forevermore!

His love for me never changes. I can do nothing to make Him love me more or love me less for He *is* love.

He is all powerful. He can defeat my enemies.

He is preparing a home for *me* in heaven where I will live with Him forever.

He is my rock, my fortress, my safe haven—I can run to Him and he will protect me.

I can trust my God—He hears me when I call.

He will guide my path—He is my beloved Shepherd, He knows me by name.

He promised that he will never leave me and will be with me until the end.

Scripture says that God inhabits the praise of his people. With all of that praise and God in the middle, there will be absolutely no room for anything negative. Praise will scatter the self-doubt and the feeling of discouragement. It is one thing to know, but another to put into action.

Slip into that garment of praise and see for yourself. It will make all the difference.

YOU GOTTA PUT LEGS
ON YOUR PRAYERS

Trust in the Lord with all thine heart and lean
not unto thine own understanding. In all thy
ways acknowledge Him and He shall direct thy
paths.

Proverbs 3:5 (KJV)

Have you ever heard someone say, "I am just waiting
for God to tell me what his will for my life is"? I have
heard this many times. In fact, I have said it myself.

In my younger years, even though I was a believer
in Christ, I went through a period of searching. I was
desperately wanting to know what the will of God was
for my life. I felt as though I were drifting without an
anchor. I felt my young life passing me by while I was
waiting. I asked everyone, "How do you know what
the will of God is for your life?" and "Do you know
what God's will is for you?" I was expecting a global
announcement from God—like "Kathy, I want you to
be a missionary in China." But I heard nothing. I so
wanted God to direct my path. After all, He said he
would and I was willing. Why couldn't I hear?

Asking everyone about this subject gave me no
satisfying answers. Pray, I was told, which I had been
doing. "What do you like to do?" was another answer
that I found ridiculous at the time. Nobody knew the

answer, it seemed. I wanted God to write me a letter, send me a telegram, something tangible that I could hold on to so that I could begin doing it. My searching continued, as there was no telegram and no letter, and I was wasting precious time, unbeknownst to me. I actually got out of church for a short while, of which I am now ashamed. I didn't abandon my faith, for I still dearly loved the Lord. I was just a floundering mess. God knew, though, that my heart was sincere, and in his loving mercy and kindness, He was patiently waiting on me, wanting to lead me, but I was too busy being aimless.

My mother said to me, "Kathy, you have to put legs on your prayers"—again, which did not satisfy me. What in the world did that mean? Nothing in the world satisfied me.

Then, I came across Proverbs 3:5 noted above. Read it again, would you? When I review, I was not trusting. I was trying to lean on my own understanding. I was not acknowledging Him in all my ways and He could not direct my path because of it. I was doing exactly the opposite of what this Scripture instructed me to do.

I began to understand that I was not doing what I already knew to do for God. I knew I was to go about doing good as Christ did. I knew I was to walk in love. I knew I was to not forsake the assembling of myself with other believers. I knew I was to pray without ceasing. I had a lot of head knowledge, but I was not putting it into action. Thankfully and finally, I began to put into practice those things again that I knew to do. Then my ever-faithful God began to lead my path, and I feel that I am in the center of his beloved will. Sweet rest.

I just had to put some legs on my prayers. Thank you, Mama, you were so right.

WHAT'S IT ALL ABOUT?

Greater Love hath no man than this, that a man lay down His life for His friends.

John 15:13 (KJV)

For years, people have wondered what life is all about. It has been written about in songs. Remember wonderful Dionne Warwick, "What's It All About, Alfie?" Well, I don't believe that Alfie knew either. And that Hokey Pokey song. Seinfeld says, "What if that really *is* what life's all about, puttin' your right foot in, etc.?" Oh, brother, we would be so doomed, right? Talk about what's the use?

But I know what life is all about. Really, I do. It is the only thing that makes perfect sense in this confusing world that is quickly swirling downward.

It's about the inspired Living Word of God that explains it to us, our map! Our GPS, if you will!

It's about the Ten Commandments that are commands that were written for our *protection* throughout life and not so that we could not have a "good time, as I have heard one young man explain them.

It's about God's sinless Son who was willing to leave the glories of heaven to live among those who had lost communication with his Father, the One True God.

It's about God's Son, Jesus the Christ, who walked among us, taught us how to love the unlovely, care for those in need, to forgive those that we hold a grudge against, to fellowship in brotherly love, who taught us how to live together in sweet harmony...*if only the fighting world would listen.*

It's about Jesus our Christ, who was *willing* to endure the most horrifying death on a cruel, rugged cross publicly so that *you* and I could have one more opportunity to accept his offer of eternal life in a home he has prepared just for us. Life with our God who loves us, Jesus and the Holy Spirit for eternity! What glory that will be! Oh, please don't miss out on this!

It's about the God Man who would rather die for you than to ever spend eternity without you.

NEGLECT

I passed by the field of the lazy man, and by the vineyard of the man who lacked understanding. And there it was, all overgrown with thorns; Its surface was covered with nettles; its stone wall was broken down. When I saw it, I considered it well; I looked on it and received instruction: A little sleep, a little slumber, a little folding of the hands to rest; So shall your poverty come like a prowler, and your need like an armed man.

Proverbs 24:30–34

Neglect. Neglect. Neglect even sounds like a negative word, and well, it should. If you are like me, if I go too long without weeding and dead-heading the flower garden, it is no longer something of which I can be proud, for the weeds and grasses will simply take over in a New York minute, and what was once a pleasure to enjoy becomes a much dreaded chore.

If I neglect my Bible reading for too long, I can tell a difference in my connectivity and direction.

If I neglect prayer in my life, I lose the power that it can have in my life.

If I neglect a good friendship, I will soon lose good fellowship with that friend.

If I neglect to come to work, then poverty will come upon me like the prowler mentioned above and my need like an armed man.

King Solomon wrote the Scripture above and the Bible records him as the wisest man to ever live. He was really right on point with this proverb, wouldn't you say? I just love the part that reads, "When I saw it, I considered it well. (He studied the overgrown field and the broken stone wall.) I looked on it and received instruction. [parenthesis mine]"

There is another area in our life that is so pivotal and must be addressed as we simply must not neglect it and that is the accepting of Christ as the Son of God and inviting him into our hearts to secure our eternal salvation. We are not promised tomorrow. What needs to be done should not be neglected and should be done today, for we know not what tomorrow holds.

> How shall we escape if we neglect so great salvation?
>
> Hebrews 2:3 (KJV)

> Forgiving Father, please have mercy on us when we behave like the man in your Word with the vineyard who lacked understanding, who slept, slumbered, and folded his hands for a season. Father, let us be like the traveler who observed, considered it, and received instruction. Help us, Lord, to be awake and aware, busy about the business that you have given each of us to do. But most importantly, Lord God, let us not neglect our souls that will forever live somewhere in eternity. Let us

not neglect so great a salvation, so full and so free.

In the name of Loving Jesus, who did not neglect us, we give you honor and glory and praise!

GOD'S JEALOUSY

For I, the Lord your God, am a jealous God.

Exodus 20:5 (NKJ)

For I am jealous for you with a godly jealousy.

2 Corinthians 11:2 (NKJ)

What? Our God is a jealous God? Why, that doesn't even sound remotely like a quality trait of the Most High, does it?

I once heard a popular TV talk show host relate that these verses made her doubt because she just couldn't imagine this as a truth about God. Oh, how I wanted to talk with her and still do.

I would like to tell her that this is a most loving trait of the Most High and one that she should be honored and thankful for in that it keeps him in pursuit of her and her eternity, his own dear creation.

The first two of the Ten Commandments read as follows:

1. Thou shalt have no other gods before me.

2. Thou shalt not make unto thee any graven image.

God is well aware that our enemy, Satan, is out to destroy our relationship with him as he hates God and hates anything or anyone that God loves, which means me and you. Satan's desire is to turn our heads to other gods and idol worship, and he knows full well that he can do it, if we are not careful and stay focused on Christ. We can make a god or an idol out of anything, really. It doesn't have to be specifically a graven image, although it could be as it often was in the Old Testament. We can make an idol out of a hobby or out of our work. We can make an idol out of the love of money. Or watching TV for hours on end. We can even make an idol out of our relationships with others. Anything that you put before your relationship with God is an idol to you. That right there is food for thought. We may not even be aware of this. We should examine ourselves on a regular basis.

God says to us in effect, "Children! My children, stay focused on me. I know what is best for you as I created you in my own image. Do not walk into the dangerous territory of what you think is another love that will lead you away from me and off the good path that I have for you and your life and your future. These relationships that you have with other gods will ultimately destroy you. I have a godly jealousy for you, for you are mine. I gave my only Son for you. These idols and other gods that you have would not and will not do the same for you. They pretend to be lovers, but they want to harm you, they want to destroy you. Stay with me. Turn away from those things that separate us. I have loved you with an everlasting love and know the plans that I have for you, plans to give you a hope and a future. I don't want to harm you. Children, stay by me for I have a godly jealousy for you. You are mine. I bought you for a dear price.

For you are mine. You are mine. You are mine."

Father, I am forever grateful that you have a godly jealousy for me. I simply love this quality about you. Thank you that you want to protect me from those things in this life that can so easily turn my head. Thank you that this is nowhere near a negative trait of yours but one that reveals your unconditional love for me. And for this reason, I am yours. I am yours. I am yours.

EXPECT AN ANSWER!

But they said to her, "you are beside yourself!"

Acts 12:15 (NKJ)

Cruel King Herod hated the followers of Christ so much. Verse 1 of Acts says that "He stretched out his hands to harass some from the church." So he killed the disciple James, the brother of John, with a sword. Scripture goes on to say that it put him in a good light with the Jews, and when he saw that it pleased them and gave him favor, he decided to go after Peter and put Peter in prison and was going to publically lynch him after the Passover. Herod wanted to make sure he was secured in the prison, delivering four squads of soldiers to guard him.

While Peter was in prison, constant prayer was being offered up by the church on Peter's behalf.

So here is Peter, in a dark dungeon prison, bound with two chains, between two soldiers, and also with guards at the door. Herod thought he was all that but he didn't know the power of our God. Praise you, Father! Dear Peter had so much peace that passed understanding that he was sound asleep, resting in the Lord, with all those guards watching him. Those guards didn't realize that they were in for the last night of their lives literally.

Scripture relays, "Now Behold, an angel of the Lord stood by him (Peter) a light shone in the prison. The angel struck Peter on the side and raised him up, saying 'Arise quickly!' and the chains fell off his hands. The angel said to him, 'Gird yourself, tie your sandals—Put on your garment and follow me.'" So Peter, does as he is told, follows the angel out not realizing this was real but thought himself to be having a vision or dreaming. Peter and the angel went past the first and second guard posts and came to an iron gate that led to the city. The gate opened of its own accord. They went through the gate and down one street, and immediately, the angel departed from him. Peter came to himself and realized that the Lord had delivered him from the cruel hand of King Herod and the Jews that were against him. When he considered this, he came to the house of Mary, mother of John Mark, another disciple—this is where the prayer meeting was taking place for Peter. Peter knocked on the door and a young girl named Rhoda came to answer, but when she recognized Peter's voice, she got so excited that she forgot to open the door for him, (bless her) in her haste to tell the others that their prayer was answered.

Darling little Rhoda. Do you know what those praying folk said to her? "Rhoda, you are beside yourself!" They didn't believe her! But Rhoda insisted, Then they said, "Well, it must be his angel!" And here is Peter feverishly knocking on the door. I can imagine him looking over his shoulder to make sure that no one was coming after him, and he couldn't get in to his own prayer meeting!

I said all of that to say this. Dear ones (myself included), when we pray, do we believe that God will answer our prayer? We are to expect God to answer! We are not just talking to the wind. Go back and look at all of the miracles that took place while God's people were praying for Peter's release. First of all, I consider it a miracle that Peter could even sleep at all. I know I couldn't. A light shines in the darkness, God sends his angel to wake Peter up and lead him to freedom. Past the four squads of guards. I don't know what their deal was. Did God cause them to go into a deep sleep? Nevertheless, they knew nothing, saw nothing, and heard nothing. The chains fell off Peter's hands. The gate opens of its own accord (we know that God opened this gate for Peter). All of these wonderful prayers being answered while the church was praying, but they did not believe until they saw Peter for themselves. Poor Rhoda. She told ya'll it was him!

People, let's believe our God; let's believe that He can answer just like He did in the days of Peter. He is the same God. He never changes. He is our Deliverer.

If you pour your heart out to God in earnest then, expect Him to answer!

IF IT BE YOUR WILL, LORD

Pray without ceasing.

1 Thessalonians 5:17 (KJV)

Missionary Paul was inspired by the Holy Spirit to write this verse to the Church at Thessalonica. Now, of course, we cannot literally pray twenty-four hours a day without ceasing but we are to be in an attitude of prayer at all times if we are believers in Christ.

I wrote a little earlier about a miraculously answered prayer of the Church regarding Peter's release from prison as he was imprisoned unjustly. God immediately answered those prayers coming up before him from the Church. My point being that often we pray and don't really expect God to answer, just as those folks didn't. But God can and does answer, when he sees fit, immediately.

But what do we do when we do not get an immediate answer? For myself, during my Christian life, I have received many different answers from God about different things. Sometimes, he has instructed me to wait, and I did, not wanting to, but I did, for years. Then he came through with something more wonderful than I could have imagined, but only much later. On more than one occasion, he has said simply no or has actually been silent on an issue that I have brought before him many times. And it seems so simple to me, in that he could just do this for me, but each time, I am met with silence. I don't understand it, but I trust him, and I expect an answer, so I keep praying about it. It may not be God's will for me regarding this issue. And I will accept it, but I feel that I am to keep praying about it, and I will.

I have had a burden for someone to come into the faith that I love and respect so deeply, and it seems the more I pray, the further away my friend gets, but I am going to keep praying for him. He may as well surrender. Prayerfully, this will happen in my lifetime. What a joyous miracle that will be! But I expect an answer. It is up to this person to submit, God will not force him to love Him and submit to His will, but I am continuing to lift him up in prayer.

God may whisper to us that his grace is sufficient for us as He did to Paul when Paul asked God to remove the thorn in the flesh from him. There has been a lot of speculation as to what this thorn in the flesh was, but God did not see fit to remove it, and Paul accepted that fact after praying about it three times. God can see further down the road than we can and knows what is best for us, so we are to trust His judgment.

Imagine your little Johnny coming up to you and saying, "Can I go play on the interstate with Billy?" And you say, "Absolutely not." Well, Johnny thinks you are so, so mean, but what he doesn't know is that you know the perils of playing on the interstate. And he does not know when you say no sometimes, it is out of love and protection for him, but one day he will. The same with God. We may go against what God instructs and may have to suffer because of it. But He knows the future and we don't, thankfully. One day, we will understand why He says no and will no doubt say, "Thank you, Father, for saying no to that prayer of mine back then. Now I understand." Or we may not understand until He makes all things clear for us in heaven. But trust Him.

The point for me is that we are to stay in contact with Him by continually being before Him in prayer. He may not answer in the manner in which we want always, but that is why we pray "if it be Your will," because, ultimately, that is what we want. We want God's will in our lives, which is, by far, the best.

WHAT IS YOUR LIFE VERSE?

———

They will be called oaks of righteousness, a planting of the LORD for the display of His splendor.

Isaiah 61:3 (NIV)

Today's devotion was inspired by a prayer group session with some ladies from my church and even surrounding churches last night, graciously and deliciously hosted in a dear friend's home. A grand night of bringing petitions before the Lord, reading of Scripture, and much needed fellowship. The verse above was read by one of my Bible fellowship classmates and was deemed as her life verse. She stated that this verse described what she wanted her life to be. This was a new Scripture to me as I have not noticed it before, and I found it so lovely and quite fitting for a life verse.

A life verse, in my definition, is a Bible verse (s) of your own choosing that most defines you and what you are about. What your goal might be for your life. A mission statement, if you will. A verse that speaks to you, one that, maybe, you feel that God gave you and is a verse just for you. This verse from the Bible can bring you comfort like no other or bring you joy when things are going right. It can be shared with others to inspire them. It can inspire you to keep on keeping on when it seems you can't make another step.

In my opinion, it is okay to have more than one life verse. At different stages in our lives, different scriptures speak to us in different ways...The Living Word, remember, Hebrews 4:12? For the Word of God is alive and active, a *Living* Word. How can you not love that? I pray that we will grow to love the Word of God more and more, treasure it more and more, and realize more and more the tremendous gift that it is.

Have you a life verse? If not, I challenge you to pray about it and let God help you choose one. It will bring more definition to your life, give you a goal for which to strive, and it will become a treasure to you.

> Father God, our Author of the Living Word, how gracious and loving of you to provide for us, not merely words on a page, but a living active letter of love to us. Create in us, Lord, a greater desire to know more about you, to be hungrier for your message so that we too can be oaks of righteousness, a planting of yours, so that we can display your glorious splendor. We pray in the Name above all Names, Lord Jesus! Amen.

THE HELPER

> But I tell you the truth, it is to your advantage
> that I go away; for if I do not go away, the
> Helper will not come to you; but if I go, I will
> send Him to you.

John 16:7 (NASB)

This, of course, is Jesus speaking to his beloved disciples, trying to comfort them because it was nearly time for his departure back to the Father. In the paraphrase, The Message, Christ says this to his disciples. John 16:4: "I didn't tell you this earlier because I was with you every day. But now I am on my way to the One who sent me. Not one of you has asked, 'Where are you going?' Instead, the longer I've talked, the sadder you've become." Then, he promises the coming of the Helper. Older translations call him the Holy Ghost, some the Advocate, some the Spirit of Truth, and some, the Holy Spirit.

I have long been fascinated and excited about the presence of the Holy Spirit. Yet I know so little about him really. I have felt the presence of the Holy Spirit many times, and my, what joy he brings to me. For me, I have not heard much in the way of sermon regarding the Holy Spirit. I am not really sure why that is. For the Holy Spirit is the third part of the Holy Trinity, the Godhead. There is the Father, the Son (Jesus), and the Holy Spirit. My belief is that the moment that you are saved from sin and become a follower of Christ that the Holy Spirit is sent to dwell within you. How I long to be a clean vessel in which he can live. The Holy Spirit quickens me if I am drifting into a sinful area in which God would not be pleased and I might be in danger. It might be in my thought life, it might be an attitude, it might be a relationship. Somehow, I get a check in my spirit and sense that I am on a slippery slope and I must aright myself. *The Helper* warns us.

But then there are times when I am in a wonderful church service or during a quiet time when I am reading the Scripture intently or even during a song service that I can feel the joy bubbling up inside of me so that I can barely sit still and I know that to be the joy of the Lord that the Holy Spirit produces in me, such an awesome and sweet blessing. How thankful I am for this in my life! *The Helper blesses us*!

Christ goes on to say in John 16: in the paraphrase The Message, "I still have many things to tell you, but you can't handle them now. But when the Friend comes, the Spirit of Truth, He will take you by the hand and guide you into all the truth there is. He won't draw attention to himself, but will make sense out of what is about to happen and, indeed, out of all that I have done and said. He will honor Me, He will take from Me and deliver to you. Everything the Father has is also Mine. That is why I've said, 'He takes from Me and delivers to you.'" The Holy Spirit can help you discern and understand more completely the Scriptures. *The Helper teaches us*.

Oh, how I love that! I love the "I still have many things to tell you, but you can't handle them now" statement. I am so thankful that God knows just how much to reveal to us and when. When He knows that we are ready. Can you imagine what our lives would be like if we did not have the Helper? Thank you so much, God, that while we cannot today have you in the flesh, until that glorious day, we can individually have your sweet Holy Spirit, our Helper.

My friend, you might not even be aware of his Holy Presence within you. If you are not aware of this amazing Gift, ask Holy God to make your spirit sensitive to Him. He will make your Christian life so much sweeter and joyful and be a very present help in time of need for He is, indeed, *the Helper.*

HOW LONG, OH LORD!

Take time to read this beautiful Psalm of David with only six verses. It is a distressed plea for deliverance and for God to draw near him again. Four times within the first two verses of this pleading Psalm, David asks, "How long, Oh Lord? Will you forget me forever? How long will you hide Your Face from me? How long will I carry this burden in my soul, having sorrow in my heart daily? How long will my enemy be exalted over me?" (Psalm 13:1–6).

This may have been a time in David's life when he was being pursued by King Saul in his effort to kill David out of jealousy. David felt that God was not smiling on him as he had done in the past, that God was hiding his face from him. He felt that he was all alone with this burden on a daily basis. But David was doing exactly what he was supposed to do. He was praying and expressing his frustration to God. God is big enough to handle our questions like this if they are asked in the correct manner. They must be asked reverently, not in anger. In my opinion, I would think that God would welcome them as these questions indicate that we are thinking and considering what the problem is that separates us from God. God will help us regain the right perspective and give us peace.

Even though the question of how long God would delay in intervening remained, notice that near the end of this passage that David's despair seems to have lifted as he says to his Faithful God, "But I have trusted in your faithful love. My heart will rejoice in your Salvation (deliverance)." David is reminded of God's goodness and how he has dealt bountifully with him in past troubles. When we are reminded of God's love and desire to have a deep relationship with us, the promise of salvation, we can end our prayer of distress with a positive note. Because we can trust God to carry out his promises of deliverance. You may question God's timing in your own life as his timing often doesn't align with ours but never doubt for a second that he is working in your life and on your behalf. He has promised and God cannot lie, as he is perfection. He is holy. He is our Deliverer. Jehovah Nissi—He is our banner. When your battle is over and you have been delivered, you will have earned the right to replace the deceiver's banner with the victorious banner of God and He always wins the battle. You can claim victory over your own personal burden or enemy through and with God. God delivered David from the paw of the lion and the paw of the bear as a young shepherd boy, from the threatening and fearsome Goliath and from King Saul and He will deliver us.

Your job is to concentrate on being a "man after God's own heart," as God said of David and do what you know that God would have you do, my friend, and our God will deliver you.

Then we can all sing that wonderful old hymn together, Palms of Victory, written in 1836. Remember it?

While gazing on that city / just o'er the narrow flood/ a band of holy angels came from the throne of God/ they bore us on their pinions safe o'er the dashing foam/ and joined us in our triumph, Deliverance has come!

THE FRUIT OF THE SPIRIT IS LOVE

> But, the fruit of the Spirit is love, joy, peace,
> longsuffering, kindness, goodness, faithfulness,
> gentleness, self control.
>
> Galatians 5:22–23

The term *Spirit* here is indicative of the Holy Spirit that dwells within a person's life when they accept Christ as personal Lord and Savior and become a Christian. *Fruit*, as it is applied here, is an indication of healthy growth in a Christian's life as evidenced by the Holy Spirit. Paul, the author of Galatians, tells us that we will produce the above attributes if we are growing strong in our Christian lives with the indwelling of the Spirit of God.

The first fruit that is mentioned is love.

When love is mentioned, the first thing that comes to mind is romantic love for most of us, but this Scripture is not talking about romantic love. It is speaking of agape love. This type of love is not a feeling. It is a choice. It is something that you choose to do. Agape love is selfless, sacrificial, and unconditional. This is the type of love that God has for his children. God chose to love us while we were yet sinners, even in our sinful state, God loved us. He selflessly died to deliver us and bring us back to himself. This is unconditional love. If you choose to love someone, you put their needs before yours. That is what Christ did.

I imagine that you love your children unconditionally or you should. No matter what they do or don't do, you still love them. Their value isn't based on what they do or don't do. They are your children and you love them. And not to say that you don't punish them when they disobey. You actually punish because you love them and long to protect them.

With love as the fruit of the Spirit in your life, you begin to really know and experience what true love really is. It is produced and grows within you, if you will allow it to develop. Practice it, receive it. Do you recognize the fact that you are loved unconditionally? Nothing you can do can make God love you any more than He already does. His love is not based on performance. Tonight, before you lay your head on your pillow, get by yourself and ponder this astonishing fact and bask in the sweetness of it for a while. Whisper it to yourself, "God loves me unconditionally. God loves me. God loves me." God loves even me. This is a gift especially for you. Won't you receive it? Accept it? Do it, won't you? Then, praise and thank Him for it and simply rest in His love.

THE FRUIT OF THE SPIRIT IS JOY

But the Fruit of the Spirit is….Joy

Galatians 5:22

Rejoice, joyful, enjoy. I so love words. I love to look up their unique meanings. I love how words can paint colorful pictures in your mind. Joy is one of my favorite words as it even sounds, well, joyful! Did you know that there is a difference between having joy and being happy? Happiness is a result of a happening, it is conditional. Say for instance, our boss saying to us, "Job well done," would make us happy. Passing a dreaded test would make you happy. Seeing an old friend from long ago would make you happy. But, often, happiness is not long lasting as it is based on external temporary events, but joy is quite different. True joy is described as an emotion evoked by well-being and contentment. It is a deeply engrained internal emotion not controlled by happenings, events, circumstances, or surroundings. Joy that is produced by the Holy Spirit in us is a permanent blessing. You can actually be distressed and yet have sweet joy in your heart. Scripture tells us that God wants us to be joyful, enjoying our lives. Jesus says to us, "I came so that you could have life and have it more abundantly." You can't have abundant life without joy in the mix. The angel says to the lowly shepherds, "I bring you good tidings of great joy, which shall be to all people," announcing the birth of Christ.

Another interesting fact is that joy is a topic often found in the Holy Scriptures. The word *joy* appears 158 times and the word *rejoice* appears 198 times. A few more wonderful examples?

Psalm 16:11 is a psalm of David speaking to God: "You will show me the path of life; In Your Presence is fullness of joy: At your right hand are pleasures forevermore."

How lovely is that? In the presence of Almighty God, there is fullness of joy, if you are a believer in Christ. I so hope that you have experienced this grand wonder.

> But at midnight Paul and Silas were praying and singing hymns to God, and the prisoners were listening to them.
>
> Acts 16:25

The Book of Acts, written by Luke, a disciple of Christ, speaks of Paul and his missionary friend, Silas, having been put in prison by the Roman magistrates who were told that Paul and Silas were teaching customs that were not lawful for them to receive or observe. Paul and Silas were beaten with rods according to Scripture, placed in an inner prison with their feet placed in stocks. Scripture says that they had many stripes laid on them, yet in verse 25 at midnight, Paul and Silas were praying and singing hymns to God. Absolutely, no doubt, they were in pain, bruised, and bleeding, in a dark, damp cell with a rancid stench all about them, singing and praying. That is not happiness, my friend. That is sheer utter joy in the Lord. Deep-seated love for their God, knowing and believing in the promises of their holy and righteous God. That is the sacrifice of praise!

Paul and Silas were in God's holy presence with fullness of joy.

> This is Peter, another disciple, speaking of Jesus Christ : whom having not seen… you love Him. Though now you do not see Him, yet believing, you rejoice with joy unspeakable and full of Glory.
>
> 1 Peter 1:8

> Your call to action? Read tonight in the Book of Acts 16:16–34. Find out why Paul and Silas were imprisoned and the miraculous events that took place at midnight as they were singing and praying as the sound of their joy rose to the heavens, Holy God came on the scene. You will surely rejoice in it!

THE FRUIT OF THE SPIRIT IS PEACE

And the Peace of God which surpasses all understanding will guard our hearts and minds through Christ Jesus.

Philippians 4:7

Peace, harmony, stillness, unity, order, calmness, tranquility.

I feel that I can say for all of us that these are words that we want to describe our lives and our household.

Catherine Marshall is a favorite author of mine. She was married to the late Peter Marshall, who was a famous minister and also an author. Ms. Marshall tells a story that I would like to share regarding her friend, Marge, and our subject of peace for today.

Marge had an experience aboard a plane bound for Cleveland. While waiting for takeoff, she settled into her seat. She noticed a strange phenomenon. On one side of the plane, her window revealed a sunset filling the sky with glorious color. But out of the other window, all she could see was a dark and threatening sky with no sign of sunset. As the plane's engines begin to roar, she felt a gentle voice speaking within her. "You noticed the windows. Your life, too, will contain some happy and beautiful times, but also some dark shadows. You see, it doesn't matter which window you look through, this plane is still going to Cleveland. So it is with your life. You can focus on the bad things or you can focus on the bright things, but I am still in charge either way and your final destination isn't determined by what you see or feel along the way."

Isn't that beautiful? We can choose how we respond. We can be peaceful and live by faith and not by our emotions. That spoke volumes to me. I know that it is easier said than done, but if we can muster up enough faith and not let our emotions rule us, then we can have a more peaceful life, knowing that God cannot lie and has promised to never leave us and will see us through until the end. The Scripture chosen for today describes to me the peace of God so completely, it passes all understanding. When a Christian who has the peace of God undergoes a trial that would ordinarily break their heart asunder and send them off on a different path, the peace of God can hold them together, and it is a witness to the world that there is "something to being a child of the living God." It is the peace that passes all understanding. The world might say, "How in the world are they going to get through this calamity?" It is the peace that passes understanding that God gives to us through his Holy Spirit. This is not to say that Christians don't grieve. Even Christ grieved and felt pain and sadness.

On a personal note, when my family experienced a sudden death, I felt unbelievable pain, grieving for myself and my whole family, the deepest sadness that you can imagine with no answers, literally, as to what happened, but I remember when I heard the news.

"Why, this can't be so. They have made a mistake." There was tragedy in my heart, deep-wrenching pain in my soul that would last for months upon months, but I went to God, the Giver of peace and comfort, and received exactly that, but I think of my boy every day and I still lean on God for comfort and peace about him for it still hurts, but I receive His peace in fullest measure. How good God is, and how I praise Him for it!

> Jesus says: "Peace I leave with you, my peace I give unto you; not as the world giveth, give I unto you. Let not your heart be troubled, neither let it be afraid."
>
> John 14:27 (KJV)

Friend, the world cannot give you this type of peace. Notice that Jesus says, "My peace I give to you." It is a gift and you can have it!

Oh! Please receive it, won't you? Let his peace flood your soul and you will never look at life the same way again.

THE FRUIT OF THE SPIRIT IS PATIENCE

> But they who wait on the Lord shall renew their strength; they shall mount up with wings like eagles, they shall run and not be weary and they shall walk and not faint.
>
> Isaiah 40:3

Patience is described as the capacity to endure waiting, delay, or provocation without becoming angry or upset. I love the above Scripture that gives insight into what we can achieve if we are patient and wait on the Lord. Read it again, would you? If we wait on the Lord, we will have our strength renewed; we can mount up with wings like eagles. I imagine this to be an eagle taking flight. If you have never witnessed this for yourself, it is an amazing sight. They have such strength. A few flaps of those magnificent broad wings and they are almost out of sight. We will run and not be weary and we will walk and not faint. Those are pretty heady promises to those of us who will be patient and wait on the perfect timing of the Lord and wait on his wisdom. From the opposite side of the camp, the antonyms of the word *patience* are agitation, frustration, intolerance, and of course, impatience.

A fine example of this is Abram and Sarai in the Book of Genesis. God had promised them a child. God instructed Abram to look up into the night sky and count the stars. "If indeed you *can* count them," he said. Then God said to Abram, "So shall your offspring be." And Abram believed the Lord. God was speaking about the coming of Isaac to be Abram and Sarai's firstborn.

But after a few years of waiting, Sarai became impatient and said, "The Lord has not given us a child. Go in unto my Egyptian maid servant, Hagar—maybe we can have a child through her." So Sarai gave Hagar to Abram as his wife. And Abram slept with Hagar and she became pregnant. After becoming pregnant, in Hagar, there raised up a spirit of superiority, and she looked down on Sarai, which did not go over well. Sarai blamed Abram for this confusion and disorder in the household, and Abram threw up his hands and said to Sarai, his wife, "Do as you wish, she is your maidservant." So Sara ran Hagar out of the house. Hagar bore Abram a son named Ishmael, but this was not to be God's promised son to Abram.

Isaac was to be the promised firstborn son of Abram and Sarai from whom a large family would follow, as many as the stars in the sky, remember?

Sarai and Abram sadly took matters into their own hands when they became tired of waiting on God. God had promised, but they thought they would help him out. And you see what turmoil it caused for everyone involved. They did not wait on God to come through. Sometimes, we create our own problems and suffer for them.

Be patient, Christians, and give God room and time to work. What he says He will do. In his own time. Isaac was eventually born, as God had promised, but Abram and Sarai were old and in their nineties! I believe that God waited until it would be physically impossible for them to have a child on their own so that when God came on the scene and performed a miracle so that Abram and Sarai could bear a child at this age, then the world would know that it was truly a fulfillment of God's earlier promise and our beloved Christ came out of that lineage,

So worth the wait, don't you think?

THE FRUIT OF THE SPIRIT IS KINDNESS

She opens her mouth in wisdom and the teaching of kindness is on her tongue.

Proverbs 31:26 (NASB)

This verse above in Proverbs is a portion of Scripture that describes a woman of worth—an excellent wife. Take a little time to read verses 10–31 of chapter 31. Interesting and humbling.

Kindness, a fruit of the Holy Spirit, is a lovely trait to behold in another person. In today's world, it is somewhat uncommon. You can actually see genuine kindness in another's eyes. A sincere act of kindness is something long remembered by the person to whom it is given and will make the giver memorable, indeed.

Just on a whim, could you offer to cut a neighbor's grass just because you had your mower out? Could you listen, really listen, intently to someone sharing a burden with you? Could you take a minute, out of a kind heart, to direct or escort someone who is lost to their nearby destination, even though you are in a hurry? Could you offer to babysit for a friend who is a single mother without being asked? Let someone in front of you in traffic with a smile and a wave? Offer to take care of a sick friend in need? Prepare some delicious soup for them?

These are acts of kindness and born from an inner desire to do something for another person, even if you know that you will receive nothing in return. People that, from the heart, perform random acts of kindness also benefit from "just the joy of doing something" for someone else.

I can say for certain that Christ was a kind person. I feel I can say with certainty that He was never harsh or rude to those that followed Him daily. I love to imagine what type of voice He might have had: authoritative, but gentle, I am sure. I believe that He talked and laughed with the children about Him, maybe even played a game or two with them. I imagine that He gently took the withered hands of the aged in his and blessed them and comforted them. Yes, Jesus was a very kind person. And we are to be imitators of Christ.

Go out of your way to be kind to someone today. A good deed doesn't have to be a grand affair. Something simple and unexpected. What is kindness? In my book, it is inner beauty.

> Have you had a kindness shown? Pass it on; 'twas not given for thee alone. Pass it on; let it travel down the years…Let it wipe another's tears…'til in Heaven the deed appears, Pass it on.
>
> —Henry Burton (1840–1930)

> Father God, remind us to be your children of worth as described in your Word with sincere kindness on our tongues for everyone we encounter, just as your precious Son displayed.

THE FRUIT OF THE SPIRIT IS GOODNESS

But the fruit of the Spirit is—Goodness.

Galatians 5:22 (KJV)

How do you define goodness as a fruit of the Holy Spirit? Benevolence, charity, good will, altruism, uprightness, as opposed to greed, mean-spiritedness, evil, spitefulness, selfishness, and unkindness.

Goodness is one of the fruits of the Spirit that should characterize us as Christians. We are "called" to goodness as believers and followers of Christ. Do you or have you had someone in your life that was simply a good person? One of those that does not have a mean bone in their body as we commonly say? Those with the spirit of goodness are so pleasant to be around. You enjoy their company as often as possible.

The Holy Spirit grows in us the fruit of goodness as we mature in Christ. I have noted this to be true of those who have walked with the Lord for many, many years—often decades, saints of God, I call them. There is just something about a mature Christian who has grown to be more like Christ as they age. The fruits of the Spirit are so evident in them, full of goodness, selflessness, and unselfish concern for others. You can almost see Christ in their eyes.

This is what we should aspire to as we mature in our faith as God graciously allows us to age.

My charming Aunt Clara, the only sister to my dad in a family of five boys, to me, was the model of goodness. She is now at home with Christ, where she so longed to be in her later years, and I miss her dreadfully. Oh, I wish you could have known her! No doubt at all, you would have loved her. She was a strong hardworking country woman with a gentleness that belied her ability to work alongside her brothers as hard as they did. She had a velvety soft voice and a loving touch. She was full of encouragement in the Lord and loved him openly with fervor. She went way out of her way for you. You never left her very modest home, in Mars Hill, North Carolina, without eating a full meal that rivals any that I have had since and you never went home without taking a little something with you: pictures, a book, home-canned goods, a recipe, her community famous freshly frozen creamed corn, topped off with a warm embrace, and the soft bidding to "Hurry back! Kathy, I love you." Oh, yes, a model of goodness. I honestly never heard her say a mean-spirited thing about another person in all my happy years of knowing her. I learned much from her as she was a good teacher. I want to be just like her when I grow up. She had the fruit of goodness from the Holy Spirit. She modeled it so humbly and so well. How I long to see her again. As I know she is waiting on me with another warm embrace.

Do you have an older person in your family life or church family that is a mature Christian with the spirit of goodness? Spend a little time with them, observe them, model them, learn from them, and tell them what you see in them as a gift from Holy God. Tell them that you appreciate their open and loving witness. It will bless the both of you.

> Father God, thank you for the awesome fruits of the Holy Spirit. May others see the fruit of goodness in us as we strive to be more like your Son who is so completely full of goodness and who Scripture describes as going about doing good. May we be contagious with your goodness and spread it lavishly and fully wherever we go in a world that is in such desperate need of it and, sadly, doesn't even know it.
>
> In the name of our Good Shepherd, we pray, Amen.

THE FRUIT OF THE SPIRIT IS FAITHFULNESS

Faithful, dependable, true companion, fulfillment of promises, steadfast, loving, trustworthy.

Why, all of those qualities remind me of Jesus, do they to you? And also are qualities that will manifest in us through the Holy Spirit as we mature and strive to be as close to Christ in his image as we possibly can be.

I am saving the Scripture verse until the end of this writing…just because. In my own personal life, the quality of faithfulness is one that I long to be remembered for and the one that I want to develop as much as I can. I want to be so faithful to my Heavenly Father that he will say of me, "I will give this special assignment to Kathy. I know that I can depend on her to carry it through to the end." Wouldn't that be wonderful if God could say that of all of us? Let's be faithful unto him so that he can trust us to help carry out his work. We are his hands and his feet, you know.

Be faithful to your mate, be faithful in your relationships in being a good friend, be faithful to your employer. If you move on to another position or company, be faithful with the confidences afforded you in the place from which you came. Don't take ill feelings with you to share with others at your next stop. In like manner, be faithful to your church. If you move on to another body of believers, don't take ill feelings with you.

Be faithful to your word. Your word speaks of who you are and what you are made of. Keep promises, keep secrets told you to yourself. If you vow the vow of secrecy to another, unless it will harm someone, you are called to be a man or woman of your word.

I remember once as a very little girl, a friend of my mother's came to visit her and the friend was obviously distraught and in tears, which would make any little girl curious, right? Well, Mother sent me outside in no time flat and I obeyed. But when the friend left, I scooted inside lickety-split to get the scoop (as if I would know what it was about anyway). When I questioned her, my little mommy stooped down to eye level with me, and with a twinkle of her eyes, she whispered to me, "Kathy, can you keep a secret?" *Oh boy*! I thought. I nodded and I said, "Yes, Mama." She replied to me with a soft smile. "Good…I can too!" At that moment, a lifelong lesson learned and point well taken and remembered. I love remembering that and have so many times throughout my life. Mother was faithful to her friend's trust, to her own personal word, and to God, which increased her faithfulness to her witness

Let's be faithful brothers and sisters in Christ, faithful to our God, faithful in our witness, faithful in all that we do as it reflects who we are and more importantly, who Christ is in our lives. Just think, one magnificent day, we will long to hear our Lord and Master say to us when we meet him face-to-face, something much like:

"Well done, thy good and faithful servant, thou hast been faithful over a few things, come and I will make you ruler over many. Enter thou into the joy of thy Lord!"

"Praise your name Holy Father, have mercy on us. How I long to hear those beautiful words bidding me into my new home in heaven by my Savior Jesus the Christ! Father, I want to be found faithful!"

THE FRUIT OF THE SPIRIT IS GENTLENESS

> Remind them to be subject to rulers and authorities, to obey, to be ready for every good work, to speak evil of no one, to be peaceable, gentle, showing all humility to all men.
>
> Titus 3:1–2 (NKJV)

In some translations of God's Word, there is a title, if you will, above certain portions of Scripture to describe what is in that particular passage. In the Letter to Titus, written by Paul, the great preacher of Christ, the NKJV describes chapter 3 as graces of the heirs of grace. I just love that! We, as the heirs of Christ's grace, are to display grace in those qualities listed as obedient, to be peaceable, to be gentle, and show humility, etc. These are outward signs of the indwelling Holy Spirit within us if we belong to Christ.

> A soft {gentle} answer turns away wrath, but a harsh word stirs up anger. [Italics mine] Proverbs 15:1 (NKJV)

Did you know that if you softly answer or speak to someone who is angry, it can actually dispel the anger in that person? The Word of God is full of wisdom. We would do well to follow its lead.

I have put this verse into practice many times in my work history. If one comes across a patient that is disgruntled and verbally displaying it, most of the time, if you are gentle with them, and discuss their concerns with them softly, often their anger will subside and you can better communicate and meet their need. But if you answer in kind and are harsh in return, it will only make matters worse and fuel the flame.

I once came across a young patient that was so fearful that she simply could not respond to any kindness, except with gruffness. She was quite angry with her situation and understandably so. She could not look you in the face. Each visit, the same scenario, and finally, one day, when we were alone in an exam room, I gently told her that I felt that I understood that she was scared naturally, and I would be too, but we were here only to help her in any way that we could, that we genuinely cared about her and wanted to take care of her. "Please allow us to help you for this is not only our job, but our calling." And she broke. She cried for a long while openly. I comforted. She allowed me to put my arm around her in a genuine embrace, and she was never gruff from that point going forward. She was very pleasant as a matter of fact, turning out to be a chatty friend. All it took was a little gentleness and heartfelt concern. A touch of sincere gentleness goes a long way. It opened this frightened patient up so that she and the staff could communicate about her needs and I was and am so very thankful for that.

Now, please do know that this is not a pat on my own back. I am simply relaying a proven example that

God's Word is true and is useful for our instruction in our everyday lives.

> Thank you, gentle Holy Spirit, that we are heirs of grace. Guide us as we strive to display the grace that should shine forth in the children of our Holy God. May we always be ready with a soft and gentle answer, so that *You*, too, can shine forth in us.

THE FRUIT OF THE SPIRIT IS SELF-CONTROL

A man without self control is like a city broken
into and left without walls.

Proverbs 25:28

Self-control, self-restraint, balance, self-discipline. All
limiting to our lifestyles? Yes, but totally necessary to
our health and well-being as well as our walk with
Christ. Try to imagine your life completely without
self control.

Would you ever get to work on time—or yet, even
go to work?

Would you spend all you had on wine, women/men,
and song and risk sexual immorality?

Would you create more debt than you already have?
Would you pay your debts?

Would you eat and drink with wild abandon?

Would you ever have a quiet time or ever read
the Scriptures?

Would you control your tongue that Scripture tells
is full of deadly poison if we don't control it?

Would you let your mind rest on any and everything
that it found pleasing, yet dangerous, remembering that
sin starts in the mind?

After looking at these out-of-control situations, if
we just let go and did as we pleased, can you imagine

the havoc it would wreak on our lives? It would make us so weak and so much more vulnerable to our enemy, like a city broken into and left without walls, completely open for the enemy to plunder and ruin us. There are so many areas in our lives that must be under control.

Think of your favorite Olympic gold medal winner. Now try to imagine the years of dedication and control and discipline that it took to achieve that coveted prize.

The apostle Paul compared his life to a race, saying I run straight to the goal with purpose in every step. I discipline my body like an athlete training it to do what it should. All athletes practice self-control with the goal of winning the prize, but followers of Christ Jesus practice self-control for an eternal prize. On accepting Christ Jesus as personal Lord and Savior, the Holy Spirit is sent by God to dwell within us. And the fruit of the Holy Spirit are these: love, joy, peace, patience, kindness, goodness, faithfulness, gentleness, and self-control. When Christ saves us, we all have these qualities in us through the Blessed Holy Spirit; they may be in different states of development, but rest assured, they are there. Notice the first mentioned is love, and the last mentioned is self-control. Love is essential and necessary to develop the following attributes and then self-control is necessary for all of the others to grow. I realized as I was putting this group together that many of these qualities are very much alike and spill over into each other in our lives. If we have love, we will have joy and peace. We will be kind and good and faithful; we will be gentle and then we must strengthen our self-control to keep the remaining fruit alive.

Dearest Father, thank you for the gift of the sweet Holy Spirit. Without Him, we would be floundering. He is our Teacher, our Helper, and we are ever grateful for Him. Would you have mercy on us as we strive to strengthen this fruit in our lives, especially in the areas in which we are so weak, for when we are weak, there You are strong. Thank You that You are so ready to help us mature and grow and long for us to be ready as we run for the eternal prize, which no one can take from us. In the loving and holy name of our eternal prize, Jesus the Christ. Praise you, Father! Amen.

AT THE PROPER TIME

Which shall be fulfilled in their season.

Luke 1:20

Zechariah and Elizabeth is a married couple described in the Gospel of Luke as being upright in the sight of God and observing all commands. But there was one thing missing in their lives. They had no children, and Scripture indicates that they had been praying for a child. But God was about to change their lives forever with a very special announcement delivered by his messenger, the angel Gabriel.

Zechariah was a priest. He was in the temple of the Lord burning incense as was customary for the priesthood. Incense was burned twice daily, and when the people were outside the temple and saw the smoke from the burning incense, they prayed. The smoke drifting toward heaven symbolized their prayers ascending to God's throne.

Meanwhile, as Zechariah was inside the temple, God's angel Gabriel appears standing to the right side of the altar of incense. Gabriel said to Zechariah, "Do not be afraid. Your prayer has been heard. Your wife Elizabeth will bear you a son and you are to give him the name John. He will be a joy and a delight to you and many will rejoice because of his birth. He will be great in the sight of the Lord. He is never to take wine or other fermented drink and he will be filled with the

Holy Spirit even from birth. Many of the people of Israel will he bring back to the Lord, their God, and he will go on before the Lord in the Spirit and power of Elijah to turn the hearts of their fathers to their children and the disobedient to the wisdom of the righteous, to make ready a people prepared for the Lord."

Can you imagine this scene? Zechariah was having a hard time taking all of this information in. He really got caught up in Gabriel's first words, "Your wife will bear you a son."

Zechariah asked the angel, "How can I be sure of this? I am an old man and my wife is well along in years."

Gabriel responded, "I am Gabriel. I stand in the presence of God. I have been sent to speak to you and to tell you this good news. Now you will be silent and not able to speak until this day happens because you did not believe my words, which will come true at the proper time."

The people were waiting outside the temple for Zechariah, wondering why he stayed so long in the temple of the Lord. When Zechariah came out, he couldn't speak to them. The people realized he had seen a vision. He kept making signs to them but remained unable to speak.

When his time of the priesthood service was complete, he returned home. After this, at the proper time, his wife Elizabeth became pregnant, just as God had said through his messenger Gabriel with John the Baptist.

Father God, I thank you that your timing is so perfect. That in itself is worthy of praise. I am so grateful for the interesting and obedient life of John the Baptist, for his love of Christ, for his fearlessness in speaking the truth, and that he fulfilled all the prophetic wonder that was announced by your messenger, Gabriel, in pointing the way to Christ as the Savior of the world, at the proper time.

Would you, please, open our hearts and minds as we learn more about Your servant John in the days to come? In the lovely name of Christ. Amen.

THE BUSY MESSENGER!

And in the sixth month the angel Gabriel was sent from God unto a city of Galilee, named Nazareth.

Luke 1:26

Oh, Gabriel! God's administrative assistant, if you will. Just sent from God to Zechariah to announce the coming of John the Baptist, now God sends him to tell sweet Mary of the coming birth of our Lord Jesus Christ. I just love Gabriel. He has a totally cool job. He stands in the presence of the Almighty, awaiting his next assignment, winging his way back and forth from heaven to earth with messages of joy at Father God's command. Wouldn't you like that?

Gabriel tells God's chosen Mary about the impossible and wonderful news that she will be the mother of her own and our Savior; he tells her that she is to name her son Jesus. Notice that God named both of these babies, Elizabeth's and Mary's. Elizabeth's son would be called John and Mary's son, Jesus. Gabriel also tells Mary of Elizabeth's pregnancy, now in her sixth month. Even though she was up in age and barren. Gabriel tells Mary, "For with God nothing shall be impossible."

Did you know that Mary and Elizabeth are cousins? That also makes Jesus and John the Baptist cousins.

When Mary receives her wonderful news, she "went into the hill country with haste, into a city of Juda" to visit her cousin Elizabeth. And Scripture tells us that when she entered the home of Zechariah and Elizabeth, Elizabeth was thrilled to see her and when she heard Mary's voice, her own baby leaped in her womb for joy and Elizabeth was filled with the Holy Spirit at that moment. Elizabeth spoke out with a loud voice and said to Mary, "Blessed art thou among women, and blessed is the fruit of thy womb." Elizabeth also "knew," *I believe from the Holy Spirit,* the oh-so-special world's gift that Mary was carrying. Did you know that Mary was the first one to carry the Gospel?

For Elizabeth said to Mary, "Why am I so favored that the mother of my Lord should come to me?" She knew it was our Savior!

What a visit that must have been! Can you believe the joyous chatter between the two of them in Elizabeth's home? About the blessing of Almighty God that was being bestowed on them. Relating to each other their blessed events to come with happy amazement!

> Holy Father, thank you for the message of Gabriel to Mary, and us, that with you, our Lord, nothing shall be impossible. Help us to hide this wonderful truth in our hearts so that when we need it the most, it will surface to our remembrance. What glory! To serve a Living God to whom nothing is impossible! We praise you, we love you, we worship you, our Almighty and Wonderful God. In the name of Heaven's perfect Lamb, Jesus.

HIS NAME IS JOHN

And you, my child, "Prophet of the Highest" will go ahead of the Master to prepare his ways, present the offer of salvation to His people, the forgiveness of their sins. Through the heartfelt mercies of our God, God's Sunrise will break in upon us, shining on those in the darkness, those sitting in the shadow of death, then showing us the way, one foot at a time, down the path of peace.

Luke 1:76–79 (The Message)

Mary and her cousin, Elizabeth, visited together for three, I am sure, happy months before Mary returned home.

Elizabeth, at this point, was full term and delivered her son. Her neighbors and her relatives heard how the Lord had shown great mercy upon her, and they rejoiced with her. Eight days after the baby's birth, it was time for him to be circumcised, and they (the people performing the ceremonial act) called him Zechariah after the name of his father. But Elizabeth spoke up and said, "Not so, but he shall be called John." And they said unto her, "None of your kindred is called by this name." They asked of Zechariah, "What would you have him called?"

(Remember, the angel Gabriel rendered him speechless because Zechariah did not believe the good news from God that Gabriel had brought him.)

Zechariah wrote on a tablet, "His name is John." And Scripture says that they all marveled. At that moment, Zechariah's tongue was loosed and he spake and praised his God. He spoke the beautiful message in the Scripture verse above, indicating his son would go before the Master, preparing his ways and showing us the way, one foot at a time, down the path of peace. Oh, how I love that.

My friends, I find that so lovely and so loving of our God. Isn't it exciting that we don't have to wonder how to live, how to have peace in our hearts, our homes, with our coworkers, with a sinful world that is growing more evil by the day. We don't have to wonder about how to make heaven our final home. The Holy Scripture inspired by the Holy Spirit of the Living God shows us the way, down the path of peace. God did not plan for us to flounder around, doubting, questioning, without peace.

How I praise him that he loves us so much that he will put us on the right path and guide our footsteps, one at a time, if we will only allow it. The gift of salvation and peace is just that. A gift! What happens when someone gives you a gift? You have to reach out and accept it. It can only be your gift if you receive it, but it is free. Praise him, it is free.

If you do not know the free pardon of sin, salvation is free for the asking. All you have to do is ask Christ to forgive your sinful nature, turn from your sin and follow him. Invite him in to your heart and life. You will see life through different eyes. You can have joy unspeakable and full of glory.

I just feel impressed to say to each one of you, that God so loves you. He knows all about you. He knows your name. He knows what you will say before you say it. What you will do before you do it. I believe with all my heart that if you were the only one in this world who needed a Savior to die for your sin and set you free, He would have endured the agony and cruel public humiliation and given his very life, solely for you, just you, only you.

God loves you so much. Let that sink in your heart and mind. Put your name in that statement. God loves "Kathy Taylor" so much that he would have died just for me. Is that not amazing? But I know it is true. I know it is real.

My heart is so full this morning. God so loves each one of you, and he wants me to tell you.

Won't you receive it?

> Father God, I may have drifted off the subject of John a bit, but I feel that this is what you would have had me say. May the readers of my words and your truths deeply and fully realize the true love that you have for them as individuals. Not love like the world gives, but you, Father, the Lover of our very soul, our Creator, our Father. Praise You for who You are, for what You have already done, and for what You will do, if we will only allow it.
>
> In grateful anticipation and in Your loving name Jesus, amen.

AN UNFORGETTABLE MAN WITH AN UNFORGETTABLE MESSAGE

John {the Baptizer} wore clothing of camel's hair, with a leather belt around his waist, and he ate locusts and wild honey.

Mark 1:6

John knew that he had been set apart by God to announce the arrival of God's Son, Jesus. John chose to live in the desert, fulfilling the prophecy of Isaiah, in the Old Testament stating that John would be "a voice of one calling in the desert. Prepare the way for the Lord.

John was different than the other prophets and wanted to be, I imagine, as he knew that he had a special mission. He dressed differently, ate differently, and had a uniquely different message to share. What was his message? "After me will come one more powerful than I, the thongs of whose sandals I am not worthy to stoop down and untie. I baptize you with water, but He will baptize you with the Holy Spirit. Repent for the kingdom of heaven is near."

John was to announce the arrival of Jesus as the Son of the Living God. He was to introduce Jesus to a lost and dying people.

John's ministry of baptism represented a visible outward sign of an inward change in a person's life.

When one decided to change, or repent and turn from their sinful life, and turn to God, one was baptized as a symbol of that inner change.

John also called it like he saw it. He urged the people to turn from their wicked ways and repent. His strong message and different manner of dress attracted many people. He was the first prophet in 400 years. No doubt, he was the talk of the town. Some came, I feel I can say, out of mere curiosity and were so moved by John's message that they went back home, a changed man or woman. John was surely fulfilling his mission, and I know that God was very pleased.

Have you ever wondered if God is pleased with you in the way you are fulfilling your mission? In like manner to John, are we introducing Jesus to others that do not know Him? As Christians, we are instructed by God's Word to witness to those that are lost, preparing the way by introducing them to Jesus, His unconditional love and forgiveness.

> Oh, Father God, forgive us where we fail You. Forgive us for holding back out of fear of rejection when we know that we should speak up for You. Give us the boldness of Your prophet John the Baptist so that we can win others for you. Speak through us, Father. Help us to be aware of the opportunities that You place before us so that we can share Your wonderful love and saving grace to Your searching world that You love so dearly.
>
> In the name of the Holy Forgiver,
> Amen

THE FORERUNNER'S HIGHEST HONOR

Then came Jesus from Galilee to the Jordan (River) to be baptized by John.

Matthew 3:13

Thinking of this biblical moment in history excites me so. How I wish that I could have witnessed this. But in my mind's eye, it is so, so real. Can you imagine what John the Baptist was thinking and feeling when Christ walked up to him and wanted to be baptized by him? After all, John knows that this is the sinless perfect Son of the Living God. The Lamb of God, pure and holy. He needs no outward sign of an inward change because he was without sin. A curiosity. John, I imagine, was probably both excited and a bit confused as Scripture tells us that he says to Christ, "Jesus, I need to be baptized by you and you come to me?"

Sweet and holy, humble Jesus. I love his answer to John.

Christ replies, "Permit it just now for this is the fitting way for the both of us to fulfill all righteousness" that is to perform completely whatever is right" (The Amplified Bible).

Why would Jesus request to be baptized seeing that He was the Sinless One the world has been waiting for? Jesus's baptism identified him with our sin and failure, an example for us to follow. This wonderful event also marked the beginning of his public ministry. Great way to begin, don't you agree? Jesus was so fully consecrated to his Father and wanted to fulfill all that was right and Father God approves.

Just try to imagine this wonderful and awesome scene. You are standing in the midst of an excited crowd on the bank of the River Jordan, and here is John, feeling unworthy of this unique privilege and honor to baptize the very One for whom he witnesses. John and the Christ are waist deep in the chilly River Jordan. John takes hold of the Lord of Glory and lowers him in to the watery grave. Scripture tells us that when Jesus came up out of the water that the heavens opened and the Spirit of God (the Holy Spirit) descended as a dove lighting on Jesus. Then, the very voice of God from heaven said, "This is my beloved Son in whom I am well pleased." Glory to God! Doesn't imagining that make you want to praise him out loud? This declaration from God the Father solidifies for us the unique Sonship that is had by Jesus and God. God was identifying Jesus as his Son. Notice this is spoken in present tense: In whom, I am well pleased. God has, and always will be, well pleased with his Son, Jesus. I can almost imagine how this made Christ feel. Loving confirmation and adoration of his Father in the presence of man. It surely must have encouraged him as he began his own ministry. Notice, too, the presence of the Trinity in this magnificent scene. Father, Son, and Holy Spirit. I simply love that.

Father, thank you for our precious and perfect role model in the Lord Jesus, so desiring to please you. Let us strive to emulate him in all that he does so that we might, too, please you. May it be so with the whole world for whom he died.

Thank you too, Father, for the humble strength that we see in the forerunner of Christ, for his willingness and desire to complete the work for which he was set apart, uniquely yours.

THE HUMILITY OF JOHN THE BAPTIZER

He must become greater; I must become less.

John 3:30

In the Book of John, one of the twelve disciples, Jesus's ministry had begun to grow. In his growing ministry, his disciples had also begun to baptize those that came to him in the Judean countryside. John the Baptist was baptizing at Aenon near Salim. There was plenty of water, and the people were constantly coming to be baptized.

A dispute rose up among some of followers of John and a certain Jew. They came to John and told him that the man who was with him on the other side of the Jordan, the one he testified about (they were speaking of Christ), well, he is baptizing and everyone is going to him.

Does this note of discord ring a familiar bell with you? It is nothing but sheer jealousy. They were trying to work John up into a state of discontent and jealousy because the ministry of Jesus was growing. But John was not focused on himself. He knew what he had been born to do. He was to tell and witness the coming of Jesus the Christ. John stopped that argument before it started with his stirring devotion to the Messiah. Read John 3:30 again. "He must become greater; I must become less." What humility! John could have easily listened to the crowd and grown jealous over Christ's growing ministry. After all, he was human. But he loved Christ and was on a personal mission commanded by his God. And he followed it to the letter so beautifully. One translation of the Word reads: "He must increase, but I must decrease."

John was okay with the way in which his ministry was headed because he knew that God's kingdom in Christ Jesus must grow and increase. Even with the growth of Christ's ministry, John still pointed out the way of Jesus and his salvation. You have to love that about John. Humility is such a loving trait and is so telling about the one that has this beautiful quality. The Baptizer is willing to take a backseat. John knows that it is not all about him. He knew it was and is all about Jesus the Christ.

Beware of those in the ministry that want to point to their own accomplishments and what they have done for the ministry. This will take our eyes off Jesus and is trickery from the deceiver. Christians, we have to stay focused in our roles as witnesses of Christ and what he has done for us. Tell those that know not of Jesus what He has done in your life and that He will do the same for them. Just lovingly and humbly tell of your own mission, as John did, and give God the glory for He must increase and we must decrease.

THE BAPTIZER'S TRAGIC DEATH

When Herod heard John, he was greatly puzzled, yet he liked to listen to him.

Mark 6:20

At this time, Herod was ruler over Galilee. His brother Philip ruled over another territory of Palestine. Phillip was married to a woman named Herodias. Herodias left Phillip and married Herod, his brother. John the Baptist had been telling King Herod that it was not lawful for him to have his brother Phillip's wife as they were committing adultery. This was a daring accusation to be made of the king. But then, John was a daring, bold, and unusual character. Having her sin exposed made Herodias furious and she wanted to kill John. Notice how one does not like for sin to be pointed out in their own life. Sin loves the cover of darkness, hidden, secrecy. Sin is directly opposed to light as it exposes sin for what it really is and brings it out into the open, out of the cover of darkness.

This is why Jesus was so opposed in his day too, because he was exposing the sin and hypocrisy of those who lived in darkness. It made the leaders angry, and instead of dealing with the sin and darkness in their lives, they wanted to destroy the Light that exposed them.

Scripture tells us in Mark that Herod feared John and tried to protect him for he knew that John was a righteous man. Read the Scripture selection again.

Herod was greatly puzzled on hearing John, but he liked to listen to him; there was just something about John that drew Herod to John's witness. Was it the beloved Holy Spirit? I believe that it was. But Herod bowed to the pressure of his wife Herodias and his advisers: he had John arrested and thrown in prison. Decision making when you are bowing to peer pressure can identify your true colors.

On Herod's birthday, he gave himself a banquet for his high officials, military commanders, and the leading men of Galilee. As part of the entertainment of this occasion, the daughter of Herodias danced before King Herod. This so pleased the King and his guests that he made a promise to the young girl that he would soon regret. Be careful, do not make promises without thinking them through. Remember that our tongues are evil and full of deadly poison and they must be guarded, according to God's Word.

Herod promised with an oath to the young dancer, "Ask me for anything that you want, and I will give it to you, up to half of my kingdom." The young girl ran to her mother and asked her what should she ask for. Herodias answered, "The head of John the Baptist."

Herodias's daughter ran back into the presence of the king and his guests and announced her wish as promised by Herod. "I want you to give me right now the head of John the Baptist on a platter." King Herod, according to Scripture, was greatly distressed but because he had sworn an oath openly to this girl in front of his guests; he did not want to refuse her and go back on his word. So he immediately sent an executioner with orders to bring back John's head. The man followed his order, went to the prison, and beheaded John and brought back the head on a platter. He presented it to the daughter of Herodias and she took it to her mother. Herodias finally got her evil wish, the death of the one who brought their sin to light, but what good did it accomplish?

She was still an adulterer, and now she had the blood of John the Baptist on her hands. Sin will take you deeper and further than you want to go.

Matthew's Gospel records that John's followers took his body and buried it and then they went and told Jesus. When Jesus heard what had happened, he withdrew by boat privately to a solitary place. Jesus, no doubt, was saddened by this dreadful news and needed to mourn the loss of his relative and beloved friend. Jesus had said of John the Baptist to a crowd, "I tell you, among those born of women, there is no one greater than John."

Yes, John had fulfilled God's plan for his life in a wonderful way. His ministry was over, but he accomplished what he was set apart to do. He pointed the way to our beloved Master, introducing him to a lost and dying world. He had the most amazing honor of baptizing Jesus in the River Jordan. I thank God for John's bold and unusual ministry. His humility and yet bold and unafraid personality inspires me yet today, and I just can't wait to tell him.

THE TOMB IS SEALED

So they went and made the tomb secure by putting a seal on the stone and posting the guard.

Matthew 27:66 (NIV)

Catch a few minutes alone tonight, close your eyes, and imagine this scene.

You are at a church portrayal of the crucifixion on Friday night before Easter. You watch in horror as your Lord is betrayed by one of his own. You watch in horror with throat tightening as the accusers spit in the precious face of Jesus, the Lamb of Glory. You watch in horror as they beat and whip him, slapping the face of your Redeemer and mocking him. He is beaten until nearly dead and barely recognizable. Then the rugged cross. Your Savior hung between heaven and earth, his own dear creation. Love holds him there. Scripture tells us that he could have called a multitude of angels to set him free, but love held him there. Love for me, love for you.

You watch with horror as they take his lifeless body down from the cross and lay him in a borrowed tomb. They post a guard and the tomb is sealed. It is over. The lonely haunting cries of Mary, his mother, fill the air.

Then, the lights dim and the crowd around you begins to scatter. You think to yourself,

"Hey, wait a minute. Sit back down! It's not over! Hey, hey wait for the Resurrection! He is alive, remember?"

But it was over.

Just like it was on that dark Friday at Calvary. My Lord was dead, and his tomb was sealed.

This was an oh-so-real portrayal of the crucifixion at my church one year. I had no idea that it was going to end that way, and oh my, what an impression it left with me. I shall never forget it. It made this horrible and wonderful event so, so real. This was real life. This really happened.

That entire weekend was like no other for me. I remember my heaving sobs on the way out of the sanctuary. Still, the haunting cry of Mary followed me out, ringing in my ears. I shared so many tears with her.

Those that witnessed this actual scene had no Scripture to give them the good news. In their eyes, it was just over. Their Lord was dead and the tomb was sealed.

DEATH COULD NOT HOLD HIM

———

But God raised Him from the dead, freeing Him from the agony of death, because it was impossible for death to keep its hold on Him.

Acts 2:24

But, it wasn't over. Not for God, not for his Son, Jesus the Christ, and, praise be to God, not for us! Our God is a promise keeper. Never, ever doubt him. He can make a way where there seems no way. And how I love him for it. Those poor, downcast, heavyhearted mourners in Jesus's day were in for the most joyful surprise of their lives! Think of it! Death, hell, and the grave conquered by theirs and our Lord, Jesus the Christ.

Matthew's gospel account describes it in this manner (paraphrase is mine):

Mary Magdalene and the other Mary came to the tomb at early dawn on the first day of the week. There was a great earthquake. God sent an angel to roll back the stone of the tomb. (Mind you now that Jesus had already risen and was gone from the tomb. The stone was rolled away merely for the sake of Mary Magdalene and the other Mary so that they could see that their Lord had risen, just as he said.)

The angel's appearance was like lightning and his clothing was as white as snow. The angel said to the women, "Fear not for I know that you seek Jesus, which was crucified. But he is not here. He is risen, just as he said. Come, see where the Lord lay.

"Now go quickly and tell His disciples that He is risen from the dead and that He goes before you into Galilee." So they ran from the tomb with both fear and great joy to bring the disciples word.

And as they went, Jesus met them and greeted them, "Peace be unto you." And they bowed and held him at his nail-scarred feet and worshipped him.

Can you imagine all of the different emotions of that one single glorious morning: confusion, bewilderment, disbelief, anger for the Roman government thinking that the empty tomb was plotted trickery, but then the relief, utter joy, hope for their future, and the delight in sharing with others that Christ's followers felt in knowing that the tomb was now empty and that their Lord was indeed alive having conquered death, for they had seen him.

Believers, we should still have that same sense of wonder when we remember the Gospel's accounts of our risen Savior and what we know in our hearts. Like those early followers of Christ, we, too, should be telling everyone what we know, sharing our joy and faith in a Savior that loves us with an unconditional love, having willingly died for us and being raised on the third day, just as He said, so that we, too, could live.

We serve a Living God! Praise his holy name.

> Father, may we never lose the wonder of it all and the promise that the resurrection holds and the glory of that empty tomb.
>
> With forever and eternal gratitude,
>
> In the sweet name of our Living Jesus, Amen.

HE'S COMING BACK!

> And the napkin that was about His Head,
> not lying with the linen clothes, but wrapped
> together in a place by itself.
>
> John 20:7 (KJV)

The Gospel of John relates that Simon Peter, one of Christ's disciples, arrived at the empty tomb on that Easter morning and going in, saw the linen clothes lying there with the napkin that had been placed over Christ's head in a separate place.

I remember in my childhood church a revival pastor preaching on this subject. He was wonderful, what they call an old timey preacher full of the Holy Ghost. He called his sermon, The Napkin Is Still Folded. He began to share a Hebrew tradition of Jesus's day. The folded napkin was a message between the master and his servant. When the servant would make ready the table for his master, he would wait just out of sight until the master was finished. If the master was done with the meal, he would rise from the table and simply toss the napkin on his plate, and the servant would know he was permitted to clear the table.

But if the master rose from the table and folded his napkin, then the servant was to wait because this was an indication that his master was not done.

The folded napkin of the Master was a message to his servant: "I'm coming back!"

Oh my, the excitement and the shouts of praise that filled my little church over the prospect of Christ's return to claim his Church could not be contained! The joy was sweet that night, hearing and seeing those old silver-haired saints of God who had walked with him for decades, shouting, "Victory in Jesus," standing up and reverently waving holy hands in praise to their God. What an inspiration they were, how I loved each one of them, and how thankful I am to have been a witness to that precious scene with tear-stained eyes. Such a beautiful memory of mine. The Spirit of the Living God was in that place and was so welcomed.

Read these next verses of Paul to the Church of Thessalonica slowly—let it wash over you with sweet anticipation and blessed hope.

> For the Lord Himself shall descend from Heaven with a shout, with the voice of the archangel and with the trump of God: and the dead in Christ shall rise first: then we which are alive and remain shall be caught up together with them in the clouds, to meet the Lord in the air and so shall we ever be with the Lord.
>
> 1 Thessalonians 4:16–17 (KJV)

THE TEACUP

A couple vacationing in Europe went strolling down a little street, seeing a quaint gift shop with a beautiful teacup in the window. The lady collected teacups and wanted this one for her collection, so she went inside to buy it. As the story goes, the teacup spoke to her and said, "I want you to know that I have not always looked like this. It took the process of pain to bring me to this point. You see, there was a time when I was just clay and the Master came and he pounded me and he squeezed me and he kneaded me and I screamed, 'Stop that!' But he just smiled and said, 'Not yet.' Then he took me and put me on a wheel, and I went round and round and round and round. And while I was spinning and getting dizzier and dizzier, I screamed again and said, 'Please get me off this thing!' And the Master was looking at me and he was smiling as he said, 'Not yet.'

"Then, he took me and walked toward the oven, put me in, shut the door, and turned up the heat! I could see him through the window of the oven, and it was getting hotter and hotter! I thought, *He's going to burn me to death!* And I started pounding on the inside of the oven and I said, 'Master, let me out, let me out, let me out!' I could see that he was still smiling as he sang patiently, 'Not yet.' After a while, he opened the door and I was fresh and free finally. Then the Master took me out of the oven and placed me on a table and got some paint and a paintbrush. He started dabbing at me and making swirls all over me. I started to gag and I said, 'Master, stop it please.' But again, he smiled and said, 'Not yet.'

"Then, oh so gently, he picked me up again and started walking toward the oven…again! I said, 'Master, no! Not again, please!' He opened the oven door again and he slipped me inside and shut the door. Would you believe that he turned the heat up twice as hot as before? And I thought, *Oh no. He is going to kill me*! I looked through the oven door and pleaded, still pounding on the door of the oven. 'Master, my Master, please let me out, please?'

"Now I could see that he was smiling, but I also noticed a tear trickling down his cheek as I watched him mouth the words, 'Not yet.'

"Just as I thought I was about to die, the door opened and he reached in ever so gently and took me out, fresh and free, finally. Then my Master took me to a high shelf and he said, 'There, my child, I have created what I intended you to be. Would you like to see yourself?'

'Yes,' I said. He handed me a mirror and I looked and then had to look again. First, I blinked. Then a gulp! And I said, 'But that's not me. I'm just a lump of clay.'

"He said, 'Yes, that is you, but it took the process of pain to bring you to this place. You see, had I not worked you when you were clay, then you would have dried up. If I had not subjected you to the stress of the wheel, you would have crumbled. If I had not put you into the heat of the oven, you would have cracked. If I had not painted you, there would be no color in your life. But it was the second oven that gave you the strength to endure. Now, you are everything that I intended for you to be—from the beginning.' And I, the teacup, heard myself saying something I never thought I would hear me say, 'Master, forgive me, I did not trust you. I thought you were going to harm me. I did not know you had a glorious future and a hope for me. I was too shortsighted, but I want to thank you. Thank you for the suffering and for the process of pain and that you were there to see me through it all the way. Here I am! Your Creation! I give you myself, Master— fill me, pour from me, use me as you see fit. I really want to be a vessel that brings you glory with my life."

> Behold, as the clay is in the potter's hand, so are ye in mine hand.
>
> Jeremiah 18:6 (KJV)

The author of this bit of prose, "The Teacup," is unknown, though I did embellish just a bit, but it has been a favorite of mine for years. Maybe it will become one of yours.

I feel that it speaks volumes to its readers with an underlying message of God using the storms in our lives to sturdy us, perfect us, and make us into what he intended from the beginning. Relax, God is in control, even when we feel that he is not. He knows what is going on and is not surprised by any event. He's just not through with us yet. Praise him today for what you are becoming!

WHAT IF

But from there you will seek the Lord your God and you will find Him if you seek Him with all of your heart and with all of your soul.

Deuteronomy 4:29 (NKJ)

Come near to God and He will come near to you.

James 4:8 (NIV)

The Scriptures above whisper to us that the Lord our God longs to be known. He wants us to be involved in a loving relationship with him. After all, he created us. Do you remember in Genesis that God came walking in the cool of the day in the Garden of Eden? He wanted to spend time with Adam and Eve, and he wants to spend time with us.

How do we seek Him or how do we draw near to Him today? you might ask. By spending time in His Word that he has so graciously given us, our Bibles. If you don't have a quiet time or a devotional time yet, I encourage you to please do it. You can start by just ten to fifteen minutes with a devotional like "Streams in the Desert" by L. B. Cowman, which is most excellent, the Gospel of John, or even the Twenty-third Psalm, which is so peaceful and beautiful. A choice time is early in the morning. You might have to set your alarm just a little earlier and get up before the house starts stirring with the affairs of the day. Grab a cup of hot coffee and settle back. You can begin with a simple heartfelt prayer for God to speak to you through his Word, to teach you what He would have you learn, and to help you to apply it to your heart and life. He just cannot resist this. He has promised to come near when we do. And He will do it. Soon, this will become the sweetest part of your day, and you will find yourself wanting more and lingering a little longer. The more you learn, the more you will want to learn.

It will become a passion.

The Word of God is like a power source. We must stay plugged into it or we lose power. So we will grow stronger, as it is food for our soul—the outer man may perish, but our inner man grows stronger day by day.

Isn't it wonderful that God has provided a road map so to speak? Not just so that we can know how to get to heaven when we die, but loving instruction as to how to live our lives on a daily basis so that we can enjoy the journey with a Loving Shepherd to lead the way. Let's take advantage of this grand privilege.

I believe we can get just as close to God as we want to in this life.

What if we were to put God first in our lives, read his Word, act it out, live for him, and honor him as our Lord and Master, then we won't have to look back at the end of our lives and wonder, "What if, what if I had given everything, instead of going through the motions?"

With love to my devoted sisters,
Kathy

HE CALLS HIS OWN BY NAME

If a person climbs over or through the fence of a sheep pen instead of going through the gate, you know he's up to no good—a sheep rustler! The Shepherd walks right up to the gate. The gatekeeper opens the gate to Him and the sheep recognize His voice. He calls His own sheep by name and leads them out.

John 10:3 (The Message)

He counts the stars and assigns each a name.

Psalm 147:3 (The Message)

Throughout Scripture, Old and New Testament, we can see that names are very important to God.

Our God of the galaxies has lovingly named each magnificent star of his creation. Think of that awesome, mind-blowing fact the next time you are under his wondrous clear night sky. During creation writings of Genesis, we are told that he named the dry land, Earth, and the accumulated waters he named Seas. He named the great expanse of sky, Heaven, separating darkness and light calling one Day and the other Night.

In the Gospel of Mark, on appointing his twelve disciples, to two of them, Christ gave nicknames, if you will. Simon, He called Cephas, which is translated Peter, or rock. To brothers James and John, the sons of Zebedee, he gave the name "Sons of Thunder." I can only imagine where this came from. Loving, but arguing among themselves, typical and very loud brothers?

God prescribes a manner of approach when we offer a prayer to him. We are instructed to come before him in the name of his son, Jesus the Christ.

The final Book of Scripture, Revelation, informs us that those of us saved by the Blood of Jesus Christ have their names written in the Lamb's Book of Life.

It has been said that a person in conversation with another likes to hear the sound of their own name. Comforting, I guess. In contrast, so often in today's world, we are assigned numbers. Babies are given Social Security numbers that are kept throughout their entire lives. We have credit card account numbers, employee numbers, on and on. Rather impersonal, don't you think?

But our God is omniscient. Webster defines this word as "the quality of knowing all things at once, universal knowledge, unbounded knowledge." We have a personal God, believers! Rejoice over that single fact alone for a moment. You are not merely a number to your Heavenly Father.

Almighty God knows you by name.

THERE IS ONLY ONE WAY

———

Thomas (Christ's disciple) said to him, "Lord, we do not know where you are going, so how can we know the way?" Jesus answered, *"I am the way, and the truth and the life. No one comes to the Father except through me."*

John 14: 5–6 (NIV)

There is so, so much controversy about this Scripture verse selection. The world, nonbelievers, argues, loudly I might add, that this is a very narrow-minded, prejudiced, and discriminating view of the way to God. The world believes that there are multiple ways to God and that they can choose their own individual ways that seem right to them. To me, that is much too risky.

But these Scriptures above make such beautiful and comforting sense. With only One Way, how could you possibly make a mistake? There is just one way.

If we could get to heaven by merely being good enough, as some believe—well, how good is good enough? What if I miss the mark and think I have been good enough when I really haven't? Who decides the level of goodness that is good enough? In my eyes, that is dangerous. Eternity is at stake.

What if I thought that giving to the poor was the way to secure my place in heaven? When would I know I had given enough? What if I thought that attending church was the way? Well, do I have to attend three times a week or four or ten, which is it? Or on Easter and Christmas, as some believe? Again, too risky, my eternity is at stake.

Religion is man reaching up for God and Christianity is God reaching down for man.

Did you know that in all of the religions in the world—Christ is the only One that was willing to die for you, to take yours and my place? "For God so loved *the world*." Is that narrow minded? Is that prejudiced? A thousand times no.

If there are other ways to God, then, my friend, Christ died in vain. Would he have endured the suffering, anguish, searing pain, jeering of the crowd, screaming, "Crucify him, Crucify him!" How heartbreaking that must have been to him, hearing those angry murderous shouts, loving them, and knowing that he was completing the work that God had given him in order to save the very ones that were mocking, whipping, spitting in his glorious face and piercing his precious side? Would God have allowed him to go through this indescribable public death if there were any other way? The answer is clearly no. Don't let the world system confuse you, don't let Satan deceive you with his lies, my friend, it is just too risky, for your eternity is at stake.

I would rather believe and live for God through Jesus and die and find out that I was wrong than to live without Him only to die and wish I had believed.

Believe Him, trust Him, accept Him as your Savior, my friend, your very eternity is at stake.

LOVE AT FIRST SIGHT

—————

At once the man was able to see, and he
followed Jesus, thanking God. All the people
who saw this praised God.

Luke 18:43 (NCV)

Luke's account of this Gospel tells of Jesus and his
followers coming near to Jericho and a blind man
was sitting by the roadside begging. On hearing the
commotion of the crowd, he asked, "What is going on?"
They told him that Jesus of Nazareth was passing by. So
he cried out, "Jesus, Son of David, have mercy on me!"
Those in front of him told him to be silent, but he cried
out all the more! "Son of David, have mercy on me!"
And Jesus stopped and commanded that he be brought
to him. And when he came near, Jesus asked him, *What
do you want me to do for you?*" He replied, "Lord, let me
recover my sight." And Jesus said to him, *"Recover your
sight, your faith has made you whole."* Scripture relays
that immediately he recovered his sight.

Imagine for a moment that *you* are that blind beggar
and the blessed hope begins stirring in you because you
have heard of Jesus of Nazareth and His wondrous
miracles. And He is coming *your* way! You must not
lose this once in a lifetime opportunity because you
know what this means. He may not pass this way again.
You just must get his attention. You can't run in his
direction. You can't even see him coming. How will he

notice you? Then you think, *I know what I will do. I will simply call out his name.* So you boldly cry out to him, having heard that he is full of mercy and tenderness. You ignore those angry harsh voices around you trying to silence you and *you raise your voice even louder and stronger. Jesus, Son of David, have mercy on me!* And he stops for you. Your heart is beating so loudly you fear it will burst out of your chest, and then you *sense* his presence and that loving voice speaking directly to you, *"What do you want me to do for you?"* "Lord, let me recover my sight," and then *you realize he said,* "Yes."

"He said I would receive my sight! He said my faith has made me whole!"

Then, immediately, something wonderful begins to happen! The great deep darkness begins to fade, then splashes of radiant light, and your first focused glimpse is of that face, that glorious, joyful, smiling face of your Healer, Jesus the Christ. The one true God. It is love at first sight.

On receiving his sight, the once blind man, no longer a beggar, followed Christ and glorified his God.

> Oh, Father, how wonderful that you can heal not only physical blindness, but most importantly, our spiritual blindness. Our Great Physician and Redeemer, may we honor you with thanksgiving all the days of our lives. I once was blind, but now, praise you, God, I see!

TEACH YOUR CHILDREN WELL

Point your kids in the right direction—when they are old, they won't be lost.

Proverbs 22:6 (The Message)

A favorite happening at my home as a little girl was getting up early on Sunday morning to go to Sunday school and church with my mom and dad. I sang in a little children's choir. I still remember the words to some of the fun songs that we sang with hand motions to go along with them. "Only Little Boy David with One Little Shepherd Sling" and our military anthem "I'm in the Lord's Army." Our audience would encourage us with praise, loud Amen's, clapping of hands, and good-humored laughter.

We had an old picture of Christ in our Sunday school class. The one with Christ standing outside the door and knocking. That particular painting was interesting to me in that it had no door handle on the outside of the door. It could only be opened from the inside, indicating that Christ could only come in if he were invited in. You must open the door of your heart to allow him in, which is profound, don't you think?

I can remember walking into the empty sanctuary early one morning and the hush that fell over me. You could just sense that there was something sacred about this place with a sweet silence. This was God's house.

Sunday was also special in that, if Mamma would allow, I could bring home a little friend to have dinner with us. We would play for hours and then head back to church that night, having had a wonderful day.

Along with those sweet memories, I also was taught some important respects to carry me through adulthood. I learned to be reverent in the house of God. Mama made sure of that one: one audible, though stifled, giggle and I was out the door to my doom. I was taught respect for the Bible, God's inspired word. I learned, and happily remember this, that those sweet older members of the faith were models for me to emulate and with good reason: they lived out their faith before my eyes; you could see Christ in them. Through them, I learned that our God is a faithful God, full of promise and provision. I learned as I became older, the value and joy of corporate worship and fellowship with other believers.

I thank my mother and father for introducing me to Jesus and starting that foundation and giving me rich history on which my faith can continue to grow.

That said, please lead by example. If you have precious children or grandchildren, little neighbor children that do not attend church, please don't just take them and drop them off. They need to know that the church is also important to you. Make time to go with them so that they, too, can have a foundation on which to build. Give them the much needed opportunity to build their own memories and strong background, because now, especially now, in this confused and crazy world, they are going to need to remember that there is a place to hide, a place of refuge, in Christ, when the storms of life grow too boisterous and strong to handle alone.

If you do this, they will rise up and call you blessed.

Proverbs 31:28

SHE WILL NEVER BE FORGOTTEN

Truly, I say to you whenever this gospel is proclaimed in the whole world, what she has done will also be told in memory of her.

Matthew 26:13 (ESV)

Would you like to make a mark on this world? Would you like to be remembered for something that you contributed to the world? Listen to my paraphrase of the beautiful story of Mary and the alabaster box.

Six days before Passover, Jesus came to Bethany. He was guest of honor at dinner that evening. Martha, sister of Mary and Lazarus, was serving. John's Gospel records during dinner that Mary took a pound of expensive perfume and anointed the precious feet of her Lord Jesus and wiped them with the hair of her head in a display of great love and total devotion. Scripture says that the whole house was filled with the fragrance of this perfume.

Judas Iscariot was also at this dinner, the disciple who was about to betray Christ into the hands of the Romans for a mere thirty pieces of silver. He was angry at this display, rebuking Mary, stating that this expensive perfume could have been sold and the money given to the poor. This was a waste!

But Jesus came to Mary's defense, saying to leave her alone. "She has done a beautiful thing to me. For the poor you will always have with you, but you will not always have me with you." Christ, remember, was all about the poor. It wasn't that he didn't care about them. In my mind, he was stating that they would not always have him to worship and love as he was only days away from his death. He continued, stating that Mary had done what she could for him. "She has anointed my body beforehand for burial. Wherever the Gospel is proclaimed in the whole world, what she has done will be told in memory of her often."

Dear sweet Mary was deeply spiritual and was always found at Jesus precious feet, listening intently, worshiping and adoring, drinking deeply of his teachings. Every chance she got. Once while Martha was fuming in the kitchen wanting help with meal preparation, frustrated enough at Mary that she enlisted Christ to tell Mary to help her.. Jesus appreciated the hard work and that Martha was busy knowing that this was important too and he said so, but Jesus, *I imagine softly*, answered her that "Mary has chosen the good part, which shall not be taken away from her." Again, at her brother Lazarus's death, on Christ's arrival to the scene, Mary fell at his feet in sorrow at the loss of her dear brother. Now, having listened to Christ's teachings so intently and realizing that his death was imminent, Mary brings her precious alabaster box to anoint her Savior for burial, not ashamed, in front of the other dinner guests and wiping his precious feet with her hair, in a memorable display of love and pure devotion to her Savior, anointing his body before his burial.

I just love this wonderful account of Mary. Wouldn't you love for your life to be remembered for your deep devotion and love of Christ? *Then make Christ your passion.*

Only one life and it will soon be past; only what is done for Christ will last.

A TORN CURTAIN

Suddenly, the curtain of the sanctuary was split
in two from top to bottom.

Matthew 27:51 (HCSB)

I love the word *suddenly* in the above scripture—
Merriam Webster defines this word as "unexpected or
all at once." A total surprise! Imagine being one of the
priests in the temple at that moment! Not realizing
that they were witnessing history in the making. A new
covenant was in the works!

Matthew's gospel gives an account of this sudden
happening. The temple of God in that day was made
up of three parts, the courts, the Holy Place where
only the priests could enter, and the Holy of Holies,
the Most Holy Place, where only the high priest could
enter and only one day a year at the Day of Atonement
to offer sacrifice for himself, his household, and for the
people. A massive curtain separated the Holy Place
from the Holy of Holies. This curtain was reported to
be 60 feet long, 30 feet wide and as thick as a man's
palm. It was so heavy that it took 300 men to lift it, if it
were to get wet. And this massive curtain represented a
barrier between God and man.

Researchers have said that the high priest had a
garment with tiny bells sewn along the bottom of it so
that he could be heard moving about within the Holy
of Holies, and on the Day of Atonement, a rope was

tied around one of his ankles so that after entering this most sacred place, if he were to die because of an unconfessed sin in his life, signified by the silence of the bells, he must be pulled out. No one could enter this holy place as instructed by God. This again was serious and sacred business. It must be performed precisely as the Law of God was written.

But on this terrible but wonderful day of crucifixion, Matthew, one of Christ's disciples, tells us that when Christ drew his final breath on the cross that, suddenly, the curtain of the sanctuary was split in two from top to bottom. That short beautiful verse makes me want to shout praise unto God. Notice that Scripture states the curtain was torn from top to bottom, signifying that only God himself could have done this.

What is the magnificent significance of this sudden happening at Christ's death?

- Forevermore, no more sacrificing of animals need be made to atone for our sin as the Ultimate Sacrifice had been made!

- No more barrier between God and Humanity! God ripped this curtain asunder so that we can come boldly, reverently before his throne of grace, and we can do this unbelievable thing because of what Christ endured on the cross, the Spotless Lamb of God.

- Christ is now our high priest and our atonement for sin.

Oh, Dear God! When I read back over this, I am humbled and even ashamed that I don't come before you nearly as often as I should and could! You have made a way where there seemed no way to reunite with us so that we could be in communion with You again. And what a price was paid! Thank you, Father, for the beautiful meaning of the torn curtain. Forgive me for not taking more advantage of this unimaginable gift. I can walk right up to You and You will see that Jesus, Your beautiful Son, sent me and You will welcome me! I can lovingly call You Abba Father, my Heavenly Father, as Christ taught his disciples when they asked Him to teach them to pray. You are my Heavenly Father. You are our Heavenly Father. Draw us near to you, Lord. In this busy, chaotic, sometimes ten-hour workday world, whisper in our ears that You are waiting, ready, available at any time we utter Your blessed name and all because of the Sacrificial Lamb and a torn curtain.

EUTYCHUS NODDED OFF

And there sat in a window a certain young man named Eutychus, being fallen into a deep sleep: and as Paul was long preaching, he sunk down with sleep, and fell down from the third loft and was taken up dead.

Acts 20:9 (KJV)

In the midst of Paul's third missionary journey, he came to Troas on the coast of the Aegean Sea. There, he visited with the disciples to share a meal with them and fellowship. They gathered together in an upper chamber. Paul preached to them, and I am sure that he shared with them some of the exciting happenings of his missionary journeys as he traveled about sharing the Good News of Jesus the Christ as well as some of the troubles he endured along the way. His plan was to leave again on the following day to continue his trip, so he got comfortable and just talked with them until midnight. The lighting in the room was probably flame-lit lanterns and Scripture says there were many lights in this upper chamber. Being on the third floor, in an upper chamber, it must have been getting a little warm with the fire lanterns and all the guests together in this one room. There was a young man, Eutychus, whose name, by the way, means "good fortune," sitting in a windowsill, probably trying to catch a cool breeze as there were no glass windows at that time in history.

As Paul was speaking, this young man nodded off into a very deep sleep and fell backward out of the window from the third floor and was "picked up dead." So Paul hurried down to his side, fell on him and embraced him, and restored him back to life through the power of the Holy Spirit. Paul then said to the people, "Do not be troubled, for his life is in him." With grateful hearts, no doubt, they proceeded back up to the upper chamber, broke bread together, and Paul talked with them until daybreak and then left them to continue his journey. Scripture goes on to say they took Eutychus home and were greatly comforted.

This story has always interested me. Of course, the exciting course of events where Eutychus's life was restored back to him, but I am fascinated too with the amount of time that these people spent together for a sermon if you will. Isn't it true of us, me included, that we sometimes don't want to give an hour or two on Sunday to God in an air-conditioned building full of light, worried that we will have to stand in line at the diner and grouse about having to go back on Sunday night? A precious minister of mine used to say to us, the congregation, "If you can't say Amen, say, 'Oh, me.'"

Paul preached until midnight, took care of Eutychus, and then went back upstairs to continue speaking until daybreak? What is that? About nine or ten hours or so and then Scripture says at the end that they were greatly comforted. They weren't bugged at Paul for having preached so long and keeping them past their bedtime. These people were still enamored with their first love, Jesus the Christ, wanting to know more and eager to learn all that they could, getting their very souls fed with the preaching and teaching of Jesus by their beloved Paul who could restore life through the Holy Spirit. I believe they were filled with excitement!

Do you think that we might be guilty of "leaving our first love" as God said to the Church at Ephesus in the Book of Revelation? Try to remember back when you first came into the faith of Christ. Do you remember how excited you were, you wanted to tell everyone you knew about him? Do you remember how you couldn't wait to read the Scripture or to go to church and actually take your Bible with you? Could it be that we have lost some of our new believer's excitement? Let's get that fire rekindled and return to our first love, believers.

Oh, me.

THE BLESSING OF AN ORDINARY DAY

This is the day that the Lord has made; let us rejoice and be glad in it!

Psalm 118:24 (English Standard Version)

I have had days when the last thing I wanted to do was rejoice. I remember one evening, after an unusually busy day here, walking to my car and thinking, "Everything is so ordinary: get up, go to work, go crazy, go home, Michael, my husband, says, 'What's for supper?' clean the kitchen, go to bed, and before you know it, you are up again to the same routine…same thing, same thing, same thing." Then I noticed a woman outside the surgery waiting room. She looked bone tired. She was on her cell phone, probably talking to a family member. You couldn't help but overhear the anguish in her voice. She was tearful and telling the one on the phone that she had been at the hospital for the last twenty-four hours. She had received dreadful news from her loved one's doctor. No hope, just waiting.

God reminded me at that moment of the tired negative thoughts I had just had about the routineness of life. He reminded me that there is beauty and blessing in an ordinary day. Life is so much about attitude and the beauty is, we get to choose what our attitude will be. If we look for the negative, we will certainly find it. But in reverse, we can look for the joy in our lives and rejoice!

"Hey, Mikey, what's for supper!"

> I wonder what I did for God today;
> How many times did I pause to pray?
> But I must find and serve Him in these ways
> For Life is made of ordinary days.
>
> —Macbeth

JESUS IN GENESIS?

For God so loved the World that he gave His only begotten son that whosoever believeth in Him should not perish but have Everlasting Life.

John 3:16 (KJV)

Most all of us have read or heard the story of Adam and Eve in the Book of Genesis many times. But have you ever caught a glimpse of Christ in this unfolding story of Creation? Scripture tells us that Adam and Eve disobeyed God's one instruction for them to stay away from the Tree of the Knowledge of Good and Evil... The Creator had given them paradise in which to live with the *freedom* to choose whatever their hearts desired, but for this one forbidden fruit. At the moment that they sinned against God, their eyes were "opened" and they realized that they were naked. They fashioned together fig leaves for clothing to "cover their own sin." But God taught them that *they could not cover their own sin*. Only he could do this and did so by making garments for them out of animal skin. There it is, his plan of salvation, a sacrifice, innocent blood shed to cover the sins of man, *paving the way for Jesus*.

Why did it have to be blood? Why did it have to be innocent blood? Because, my friend, sin is oh-so-serious business in the eyes of our Righteous God. He will not wink at sin and look the other way because He loves us so much. And we would want it no other way because sin separates us from Him, our beloved Creator. We want righteous justice in our world and He is our Righteous Judge. Adam and Eve were banished from their home, their paradise, and separated from their God because of sin. Our Creator wants us to be one with Him, and to reunite us, it took this drastic measure.

So because of His great love, the only way to cover our sin was to give His one and only Son, sinless, innocent, to die in our stead. Jesus the Christ. And praise Him, Jesus was willing to do it! Praise Him today for this people for because of it, we can have eternal life!

> What can wash away my sin?
> Oh, precious is the flow, that makes me white as snow!
> Nothing... but the Blood of Jesus.
> In part
>
> —Robert Lowry (1876)

GET LOST!

For whosoever would save his life shall lose it: and whosoever shall lose his life for my sake shall find it.

Matthew 16:25 (ESV)

Is your life satisfying to you? Have you ever asked yourself, "What on earth am I here for?" Do you feel that you are getting out of life all that you should? Or is there a little nagging something that is missing?

The Scripture above, spoken by Christ, teaches us that in order to have a fulfilling and satisfying life, we must lose our life in him. What does it mean to lose your life for the sake of Christ?

If we focus on ourselves only and constantly say, "But what about me?" then we are shortchanging and cheating ourselves out of the life that he intended for us. After all, life is not all about me or you.

I believe that the Bible teaches that we are to be imitators of the goodness in Christ's life. Scripture tells us that "He went about doing good" (Acts 10:38). Jesus was not one to put himself first. He had the heart of a servant. Christ said that whoever wants to be great among us must first be our servant. Whoever wants to be first must be slave of all. He said of himself in Mark 10:45, "For even the Son of Man did not come to be served, but to serve, and to give His Life as a ransom for many."

I love that. The fact that he knew what his life was about. He is telling us in this beautiful scripture what he came to earth for. He knew why he was here and went about getting the job done. Out of his great love, I believe that Christ found joy in serving others.

For me, I am still learning that if I take my mind off myself or lose myself and change my focus to the need of someone else and act on it, as Christ did, then my mood begins to change. I become more lighthearted and joyful when I am serving someone else. When I am doing what Christ instructs me to do, I am more content. It is freeing. After all, it is not all about me.

So if you want to feel that your life is making a difference in this world, if you want to find your life, then "get lost."

Get lost in imitating the beautiful, self-sacrificing, giving, and loving life of Jesus the Christ and his teachings about serving others, act it out, do it because he instructs you to, ask him to help you, do it because you love him, and if you do, you will find your life and know what you came to earth for.

CAUGHT IN THE VERY ACT

"Teacher, this woman was caught in adultery, in
the very act. Now Moses, in the law, commanded
us that such should be stoned. But, what do you
say?"

John 8:3–5 (NKJV)

Christ was sitting in the temple, teaching the crowds,
when all of a sudden, the religious scholars and
Pharisees drag in a woman, probably scantily clad, with
disheveled hair, and noisily struggling for freedom. Her
accusers interrupt Christ and the crowd and hurl her to
the ground. No doubt she was in tears and humiliated
at having been found out, not to mention her sin being
revealed to the crowd that included Jesus, the Christ.
Her accusers go on to question Jesus about this finding,
stating that they caught this woman in the very act of
adultery reminding him that Mosaic Law instructed
that such should be stoned to death. What was the
motive behind this commotion? Scripture adds that the
scholars and Pharisees were trying to trap Jesus into
answering so that they could have a reason to bring
charges against him.

But the accusers left out a vital part of the scene.
You can't commit adultery by yourself. Where was the
man? The accusers only declared part of the Mosaic
Law. According to the Book of Leviticus, in the Old
Testament, both the adulterer and the adulteress were

to be put to death. One commentary that I read offered that the accusers were not really interested in enforcing the Mosaic Law as they had another motive: they really wanted to stone Christ. If Jesus had said, "Yes, stone her.," then his teaching and message of graciousness and forgiveness would never be accepted by his followers. If he said no, then he would be openly breaking the Mosaic Law and would be subject to arrest, which is what they really wanted.

How did Jesus respond? How interesting in that he bent down to the ground and began writing in the sand with his finger. Scripture does not tell us what he was writing. I have often wondered if he was writing out the other nine commandments in the Mosaic Law. Was he writing the name of the just as guilty man, the adulterer? Was he writing out the names of the accusers and some of the sinful areas in their lives?

After continued questioning, Jesus stood up and said to them, "If anyone of you is without sin, let him be the first to throw stones at her." Then he stooped to the ground again and continued writing. The accusers then began to walk away one by one, dropping the choice stones that they selected to the ground with a dull thud, till no one was left but Christ and the adulteress woman. "Woman, where are thine accusers? Has no one condemned you?" She replied, "No one, Master." Then Jesus replied to her, "Neither do I condemn you. Go and sin no more."

Please note that Jesus did not condone her sin. He didn't ignore the Mosaic Law. He was going to the cross to pay the penalty for her sin, her partner's sin and *our* sin. John 3:17 in the King James version reads, "For God did not send His Son into the world that He might condemn the world, but that the world through Him might be saved."

> Father God, thank you so for your loving gift of forgiveness, and for your Word that teaches us to sin not, but if we do sin, that we have a priest friend in your presence: righteous Jesus who died for the sins of this whole world. We know we can never repay you and will be indebted to you throughout eternity where we will bow our unworthy heads and declare that Jesus did it all. Praise your holy and wonderful name, Father, how we love and adore you!

FATHER KNOWS ME BEST

Listen, my son, to your father's instruction and do not forsake your mother's teaching. They will be a garland to grace your head and a chain to adorn your neck.

Proverbs 1:8–9

This lovely proverb exhorts its readers to embrace wisdom. It is wise to heed wisdom.

My darling dad is now ninety-six years old and as precious as they come. We have had many, many loving discussions about the Word of God and Jesus. We have devotions together on Saturdays. We learn together. We pray together. We sing together. We worship together. He plays hymns on his guitar for me. What a gift God has given to me! In my eyes, though they might be slightly prejudiced toward him, my dad, is a very wise man. He loves the Lord with every fiber in his being, is not afraid to witness to strangers, even today, bidding them to "come with me to the best church in the country." He is a prayer warrior. He has taught me so much, comforted me when I had doubts, and strives to live before others what he preaches. He is respected and loved by all who know him. He prays for me daily, which I consider another precious and priceless gift—to hear him bring me before the Lord is a humbling and comforting blessing, indeed. My, what a treasure! There is softness in his voice as he prays as if speaking to a dear and close friend, because he is. He has grown in the Lord now for sixty-five years or better. The longer dad serves him, the sweeter he grows.

I remember as a young girl, living at home still, I enjoyed listening to a fairly famous minister who blessed me so. Then, to my horror, this minister was caught up in a very public scandal. I remember crying and being so distraught over this, disappointed and embarrassed by this public betrayal of Christ in one whom I had trusted and had been so blessed by his ministry. I questioned my father to ask *how could I* have been blessed by this person who obviously had great sin in his life. I was so terribly confused and doubting my own faith. My father comforted me so much that day and it put things back into perspective. He gently said, "Kathy, it is the Word of God going forth that blesses you, not this man. He will have to answer for his sins, but the blessings you have received came from the Lord, your God." Blessed comfort.

In another remembrance as a young girl, Dad comforted me. I am a bit on the shy side. I can remember talking to Daddy about how crowded heaven would be, and I was afraid that I would not get to have any time alone with Jesus. Dad softly and wisely reminded me, "Kathy, you get to spend time alone with Him now, don't you?" And like a light bulb going on, I thought, *Well, yes, I guess I do!* I get to spend time with Christ alone through his Holy Spirit at any time I like. We both agreed that we did not know quite how this would work in heaven, but it must be more glorious there! Blessed comfort.

My father is such a blessing to me. He is the "picture" of God that loves unconditionally. Daddy does not always agree with my choices, and I have been punished for an occasional bad choice, but he loves me in spite of them. Same with God. I am always welcomed home by my earthly dad. He is always glad to hear from me or see me. He is full of wise counsel. He prays to the Father for me and about me. In this manner, Dad has made it easy to fall in love with Jesus as my Heavenly Father as he has modeled Him so well as an earthly father.

My friend, if you have not had the blessing of a good relationship with a Godly earthly father, please let Jesus fill that lonesome void and be your Heavenly Father. He will fulfill all that your heart desires in a dad. And He is willing and eagerly waiting. Just call on Him. He will answer.

I know it. Scripture tells us, "Listen to your Father's instruction," for the Father knows you best.

DO YOU LIVE LIKE THE KING'S KID?

And if ye be Christ's, then are ye Abraham's seed and *heirs* according to the promise.

Galatians 3:29

Do you know who you are in the eyes of God? Have you have accepted Christ as your Savior, inviting him in to your heart and life, asking forgiveness of your sin? If you have taken this necessary step then, by nature of birthright, and being born again, you are born into the family of Almighty Wonderful God! Birthright is described as a particular right of possession or privilege one has from birth. We call our Christian friends brothers and sisters in Christ because we are all part of the family of God because loving God is *our* Father.

But do we live like children of the Most High? This is never to say that we are pious and think ourselves better than others and mistreat others. We are to treat others as our Heavenly Father treats us with loving kindness and forgiveness. We are just to remember "from where we came."

Jesus himself said, "Fear not, little flock, for it is your Father's good pleasure to give you the kingdom."

In rereading the story of the prodigal son, I focused on the brother's jealous reaction. In my younger years, I felt a bit sorry for him. But now, on examining further, this brother was angry with his father, feeling sorry for himself. He didn't want to forgive his brother who had been lost and now found—after going out, squandering all that he had, and now he wants to slink back home like nothing had ever happened. And he told his father so. But the wise and loving Father explained to his unforgiving son in this manner. "My son, you are with me all the time, everything I have is yours." The son failed to recognize that he was still in the wealth of his father's love and care. He had no right to be jealous of his brother. He could have thrown a lavish party for his friends at any time he wanted, and I am sure with the father's blessing. He had all that he needed at his right hand with all the provision of his father that he could possibly ask for, yet he did not live as though he did. He had the wrong mind-set. He was missing out on his father's blessing and not taking advantage of his rightful position.

Brothers and sisters in Christ, we are to remember whose we are. We belong to the King of kings and Lord of lords. He is our Abba Father. We can go to Him at any time we choose and He will always welcome us. Doesn't it give you joy when you can give your children something that you know that they want? And you give it for the sheer joy of seeing their joy? I believe it is the same way with God. So, little flock, let's take advantage of our rightful position in the family as heirs of Jesus Christ. He is with us all the time. We are children of the King!

WHAT ON EARTH IS LIVING WATER?

———

Today, I believe most of us take clean water for granted. I know that I do at times. But when I am consciously aware, going to my one of clean faucets in my own home for a cool drink to quench my thirst—with as much as I want, anytime I want, I think of what a majorly huge blessing that is and am so very grateful. When you lift that glass of cool water to your parched lips, why, it tastes sweeter when you consider what a blessing it really is and from where it came.

We water the lawns whenever we please, wash the car, and leave the water running. There are folks that take marathon showers. Hey, I know one personally. For most of us, water is so very abundant and available to us. But not so in the sandy desert and dry climate of Jesus's day.

For instance, consider the biblical story of the woman at the well. This woman of Samaria had the duty of hauling a large clay pot to Jacob's distant well, filling this jar with the needful water, and hauling it back to her home every day.

The Gospel of John, chapter 4, teaches us that Jesus and his disciples were on a journey. Jesus was tired and stopped at a well in Samaria. The disciples had gone into town to buy food. A Samaritan woman was making her daily journey to the well to draw water. When she arrived, she saw Jesus and he said to her, "Will you give me a drink?" The Samaritan woman recognized him as a Jew and she responded. "You are a Jew and I am a Samaritan woman. How can you ask me for a drink?" (She asked this question because there was racial hatred between the Jews and the Samaritans, but not so with Jesus.) Jesus replied to her, "If you knew the gift of God and who it is that asks you for a drink, you would have asked him and he would have given you living water." The woman responded, "Sir, you have nothing to draw water with and the well is deep. Where can you get this living water?" Jesus answered her, "Everyone who drinks this water will be thirsty again, but whoever drinks the water I give will never thirst. Indeed, the water I give him will become in him a spring of water welling up into eternal life."

The woman responded, "Sir, give me this water so that I won't get thirsty and have to keep coming here to draw water."

The woman of Samaria misunderstood. She thought that Christ was speaking of drinking water that satisfies our bodies' thirst. But Christ was speaking of the Living Water that nourishes the inner man and enables us to bear fruit. The Gospel.

A little further in John's Gospel chapter 8, Jesus is at the Jewish Feast of the Tabernacles on the last and greatest day. He stood up and said in a loud voice, "If anyone is thirsty, let him come to me and drink. Whoever believes in me, as the scripture has said, streams of living water will flow from within him." By this, he meant the Spirit, whom those who believed in him were later to receive.

So the living water of which Christ spoke is a symbol of the Spirit of God. Anyone who drinks of this living water shall never thirst again.

So if you want your thirst for things of God quenched permanently, come to the bottomless well of this Living Water and drink deeply, my friend.

THE BREAD OF LIFE

I am the living bread which came down from heaven: if any man eat of this bread he shall live forever: and this bread that I will give is my flesh, which I will give for the life of this world.

John 6:51 (KJV)

On a physical level, have you ever had a taste for something, but you just couldn't figure out what particular food it was that would satisfy you? You may go through several food items before you finally get what you are looking for until that particular hunger dissipates.

On a spiritual level, there is a certain hunger in life that is simply like no other. Physical nourishment cannot satisfy it. This unique hunger is a spiritual hunger. It is a longing for the natural things of God, our Creator. God has created each of us with an inward hunger for a relationship with him, with an emptiness that only God himself can satisfy and fill. One might not even recognize this desire as a spiritual hunger, but may see it as a searching for something in life that satisfies. Maybe they hop from job to job before they find the one in which they are happy. Or maybe someone might say, "I just married the wrong person," when wanting to end their troubled marriage or if they meet another with whom they want to be married and think they would be happier. Or it may manifest as a lonesome longing that being in a crowd of friends cannot satisfy. Something is just not right.

In trying to satisfy this longing themselves, an expression from years ago was "I am just trying to find myself." Or, "I am trying to discover who I really am." Those searching would use these expressions to compensate for breaking a commitment. It made them feel as if their searching would be seen as less hurtful and harsh if they turned the blame on themselves. But it is not in another person in whom you will satisfy this deep longing.

In reality, it is a relationship with God for which we are longing. There is a deep-seated desire that nothing *in this world* will satisfy no matter how long or how hard we try. One could live a lifetime with this spiritual hunger without fulfilling this need, if they never admit that it is Jesus for whom they long.

But once one has partaken of the Bread of Life, their deep inward hunger is satisfied and feeding nourishes them as they grow in Christ, bearing fruit.

Christ rightly claimed to be this unique "Bread of Life." All that come to him have their hunger and thirst satisfied.

So get into the Word of God. Come to the table, come hungry, and take your fill.

Bread of heaven, thank you for the nourishment and sustaining strength that only you can supply and that we are welcome to take our fill. You, my Father, are all we need.

In the satisfying name of Jesus, the Bread of Life, Amen.

WHO ARE YOU LOOKING FOR?

———

Whom seekest thou?

John 20:15 (KJV)

A baby in a manger?

Born of a virgin in Bethlehem of Judea? Mary's boy child wrapped in swaddling clothes, lying in a manger?

The One of whom a host of angels declared in announcing his birth, Glory to God in the highest and on earth, peace, goodwill toward men?

The young One who astonished the priests in the temple with his teaching knowledge of God?

The young carpenter who learned his father's trade?

Are you looking for the One who turned the water into wine?

The blind-man Healer?

The leper-cleansing Man of Galilee?

Are you looking for the Sea Walker?

Or for the One whom even the wind and the rains obey?

The One that made the lame to walk and the dumb to speak?

Are you looking for the Forgiving One who lovingly washed his betrayer's feet?

For the grieving sympathetic One who cried at the death of a friend?

For the One who raised the dead to life?

Are you looking for the One who fed the 5,000 with a few loaves of barley bread and a couple of fish? With *twelve baskets* left over?

Or are you looking for the Way Maker, the Rose of Sharon, the Lily of the Valley, the Bright and Morning Star? The Altogether Lovely One?

Are you looking for the Good Shepherd who willingly died for his flock? The One who conquered death, hell, and the grave? The Risen Savior?

Are you searching for the Loving One to forgive your sin, saving you from a sinner's hell and that will stick closer to you than a brother?

If you are seeking all, dear one, look no further for your long-awaited search is finally over.

You will find all of this and more untold beauty in the person of Jesus the Christ, the Son of the Living God.

Praise his holy and wonderful name, for it is Jesus you seek!

WHATEVER IS THE GREAT COMMISSION?

> Then the eleven disciples went to Galilee, to the mountain where Jesus had told them to go. When they saw Him, they worshiped Him, but some doubted. (This event was after the Resurrection.) Then Jesus came to them and said "All authority in heaven and on earth has been given to me. Therefore go and make disciples of all nations, baptizing them in the name of the Father and of the Son and of the Holy Spirit, and teaching them to obey everything I have commanded you. And surely I am with you always, to the very end of the age." [Parenthesis mine.]
>
> Matthew 28:16–20 (NIV)

The word *commission* is described as an authoritative order, a charge or direction.

The above verses are the last directive given to Christ's disciples (and the church) before his ascension back to the Right Hand of God. Our last assignment as given to us by Christ. What a comfort is given in the last sentence, "And surely I am with you always, to the very end of the age." That should give us great confidence as we fulfill this last request of us by our Lord and Master. We are to witness what we have seen and heard and learned about God the Father through

Jesus, his Son, making disciples of all nations. We are to encourage baptism in the name of the Father and the Son and the Holy Spirit. Notice he did not say only make disciples in your neighborhood or on your job, his instruction to us was to witness to all the world, i.e., world missions. Teaching them to obey and observe all that he has commanded us.

So herein lies the rub with the world, who insists on finding their *own* way. The world, loudly I might add, wants us to stop "shoving our religion down their throats." By the way, it is not religion that we are speaking of, but a relationship, a personal relationship with Christ. But we cannot stop talking about this, dear hearts, as this is the very essence of Christianity. The witness. As this is our last instruction from Christ, we, as believers, should tell you that there is no other way to God but through him, Jesus the Son. So we would be remiss were we not to tell you that you cannot get to the Living God through Buddha or Hare Krishna or the Dalai Lama. That is a grave misconception with which the deceiver blinds you.

I must declare Jesus as the Door to you as described in Scripture. I must tell you that he is the Gate. I must tell you that Jesus is the Way, the Truth, and the Life. I must tell you that Jesus is the Son of the Living God sent to us by God so that our relationship could be reinstated through him, so that we can claim heaven and miss an eternal hell. I must tell you because I love you. I must tell you because God loves you and he wants me to tell you.

So, believers, we cannot stop telling the nonbelieving world about Jesus simply because they do not want to hear it. It must be told so that they can escape the fires of hell. We must tell them that there is danger up ahead for them. We must tell them we have found a friend in Jesus. We must tell them that they are being deceived and are being cheated out of their birthright and a wonderful relationship with God. We must tell them that there is a hell to shun and a heaven to gain.

We must tell them that there is salvation in Christ. We must not hound them; we must not behave as a crazy person screaming at someone in their face that they are bound for hell. We must not judge, for we are not the Judge. We must not push. We must relay the fact in a loving caring manner as Christ did. The fact that God, in his great love for them, died to save them. Just lovingly plant the seed and the Holy Spirit will do the wooing to himself. We are to be witnesses as to what we have seen him do in our own lives. We cannot force them to choose Christ. Even Christ won't *force* them to choose him. It is their choice. It is called free will. But we must tell them, for He commands it and He promised to be with us always to the end.

> Praise you, our Father, for that oh-so-comforting fact. Knowing that you are forever with me gives me greater confidence to lovingly reach out to a world that does not know you. We don't want to drive someone further away from you. Allow us to represent your humble Spirit and loving kindness to those who are so

desperately in need of you and that they may see you in us. May we be your effective soul-winning witnesses until the glad day you come back to receive us to yourself. In your Holy Name, I pray. Amen.

LISTEN CLOSELY FOR GOD WHISPERS

And he said, Go forth, and stand upon the mount before the Lord. And , behold, the Lord passed by, and a great and strong wind rent the mountains, and brake in pieces the rocks before the Lord; but the Lord was not in the wind; and after the wind an earthquake, but the Lord was not in the earthquake: and after the earthquake a fire, but the Lord was not in the fire: and after the fire, a still small voice.

1 Kings 19:11–12 (KJV)

Have you ever had the Lord whisper to you? You know God can be heard in a church service or a Christian concert, but don't neglect to look for him in the quiet moments. He has revealed himself in many miraculous ways, but the gentle whisper of God is oh so sweet, holy, and personal, and miraculous too.

I recall a moment when I was moving into our current home. I was alone in the kitchen busily unpacking, with the radio playing softly in the background. Just all of a sudden, I became aware of the warmest and most wonderful light, *a splash of God light*. It made me stop in my tracks. I realized then it was the setting sun, but I tell you a truth, that those soft but brilliant colors of rose, golden peach, fuchsia were inside the room with me. They simply filled the room. I could see the colors on my bare arms. It lasted for a few wonderful, but fleeting moments. I was spellbound. I hurried to the window to see the most stunning sunset I have ever seen in my life. It was just breathtaking. I have lived here for better than twenty years and I have never seen it as glorious since and I have looked and tried to catch it again.

In my mind, it was as if God were speaking softly to me, catching my attention. "Slow down a little, Kathy, and spend a precious moment with me. This sunset is just for you. Bask in my glory for a bit." And I did. He refreshed me, and I have hidden that moment in my heart and pray that I never forget it. Oh, the sweetness of a still moment between you and God is indescribable. Pray that God will make you aware of his still small voice and then…brace yourself for something wonderful.

> Holy Father, thank you for the precious few "all of a sudden" moments in my life that have made it so sweet. Thank you for loving me so much and drawing me to witness for myself your unique and divine creation. *Bring us all to an awareness of you*, Father, in those holy and delightful moments when you catch us off guard.

I'M NOT HOME YET

He has made everything beautiful in is time. *He has also set eternity in the hearts of men.*

Ecclesiastes 3:11 (NIV)

Do you ever think about heaven? I mean, really think about it and long for it? Do you ever get excited with the anticipation of going home? Read in the Scripture sometimes all it has to say about this most exciting and promising real live place and it will make you homesick for heaven.

We were designed by Creator God so that we could live for eternity. According to Ecclesiastes, he has placed eternity in our hearts, a desire to live for eternity. Eternity is defined as infinity, having no end, timelessness.

It is interesting to question others to find out what their idea of heaven is. Most of these are not scripturally based, mind you, but interesting. A friend of mine believes that it will be like one long church service, and while I truly love church, that is not my idea of heaven, is it yours? Another idea I can remember from a cartoon as a little girl is the ideation of people floating around on puffy white clouds playing harps all day. Boring! I personally believe that we will have lots of things to do: worshiping, singing, work assignments. I believe it will be a place of order and calm. Take your own little survey and ask people what they believe heaven to be;

you will be surprised at all of the different ideas that they come up with.

Mind you, I am no expert on heaven, but according to Scripture, it will be well worth the wait. Can you imagine, first of all, actually getting to meet Christ? I mean face to glorious face? I want to kiss the scars on his hands. They were for us, you know. I want to bow before him and worship him in person. I want to whisper to him how I love him and how I thank him for what he did for me. Then my mom? I can't wait to put my arms around Mother again. I fully believe that I can and will. My Thomas. You know, Scripture tells us that we will know as we are known, which means to me, that I will recognize those in heaven that I have known here on this sweet earth. I have never been much on reunions here on earth, but glory to God, what a glad reunion day that is coming our way!

Then, oh, the beauty of it as described in Scripture! A city built foursquare, gates of real pearl, layer on layer of gleaming precious stones, streets of pure gold, the River of Life, the Tree of Life, the Throne of our Living God with Jesus seated at his right hand. The angels! Can you imagine the sounds that we will hear? Oh my word! And, beloved, that is a mere smattering of what we have to look forward to. Scripture tells us in 1 Corinthians, in my paraphrase, "Eyes have not seen, nor ear heard, neither has entered into the heart of man the things which God has prepared for those of us who love him." That means we cannot even begin to imagine what is in store for us! I think about the beauty and majesty of places around the world and it boggles my mind to try to think about heaven, created by God with the key word being Creator!

And there will be peace. Oh, glory to God and praise him. Finally peace in heaven. Thank you, Father! No more pain. No more suffering. No more exhaustion, no more crying. He will wipe away all our tears! No more death! No more sin, no more deceiver. No more need for cancer centers, hospitals, emergency rooms, rest homes. No more separation from our loved ones! Halleluiah to the Lamb of God! For the former things are passed away and all things are become new. There will be joy forevermore. For eternity! Thank God that he has prepared a place for us, won't you? A prepared place for a prepared people. God's people. So that where he is, there we can be also. Oh, just the thought of it makes my glad heart rejoice!

Do I really believe all of this stuff? Oh, yes, yes! With every fiber of my being. I know it is true.

Mind you now, I love it here! I do love this world, I love my husband, my family, my job, my coworkers, my friends, my church family, the Yada girls, I love all that God has so graciously and bountifully given me here on this gorgeous earth. All I know is…I'm not home yet.

> Sweet Holy Father, when I remember your Word that tells us that foxes have holes and the birds of the air have nests, but the Son of Man had no place to lay his head. I am even more amazed at how you have prepared and have met our needs here, our beautiful earth, our homes, yet you had no place in which to really rest your precious head. To think that you would

go even further and create our final home with us in mind and give us a scriptural glimpse of what it might be is so unbelievable, yet I do believe it. And I am already thankful. Glory is coming! In this sinful world with trouble on every hand, tremendous sadness, grief, child abuse, hatred among nations, hatred of people within their own race, why the hope of heaven and your living with us forever, makes me want to keep on keeping on for you. But until that wonderful homecoming day, Father, thank you for the hope of glory! Praise your beautiful and wonderful name! You provide our every need— thank you for the hope of eternal glory, Lord. I simply can't wait until you welcome us all home, Father…Amen.

How beautiful Heaven must be
Sweet Home of the happy and free
Sweet Haven of rest for the weary
How beautiful Heaven must be

WORSHIP HIS MAJESTY

> In the year that king Uzziah died I saw also the Lord sitting upon a throne, *high and lifted up* and his train filled the temple. Above it stood the seraphims; each one had six wings; with twain he covered his face and with twain he covered his feet and with twain he did fly. And one cried unto another, Holy, holy, holy is the Lord of hosts: the whole earth is filled with His glory.
>
> Isaiah 6:1 (KJV)

Majesty, grandeur, splendor, mightiness, supreme authority.

The word *majesty* is defined as "impressive stateliness, dignity, or beauty. Royal power."

The above scripture is spoken by the prophet Isaiah upon seeing a vision of the Lord on his throne. Note the sacred worshipful "sound" of this verse. Do you think that sometimes we *forget just who God really is*? Do we become too casual in our talk of him? The Big Boss in the sky. The Good Lord will help you. The term "Good Lord" is redundant and superfluous. The "good" is unnecessary.

He is Sovereign, the Supreme Ruler. Omnipotent, he is all powerful. Omnipresent, he is everywhere at once. Omniscient, he is my all-knowing Lord.

While I recognize and cherish the fact that the Lord is *my friend*, I also want to be mindful of his deity, his divine status. He holds my very life and breath in his hands. He means what he says. He commands me to obey. He gives me the choice, but if I am disobedient to his will and command, I will suffer the consequences. This amazes me yet, but as close as God and Moses were, Moses disobeyed God and was not allowed into the Promised Land to which he led God's people for years across the desert. He disobeyed and God punished him. God allowed the people in, but not their leader. He did not allow Moses to set foot into the Promised Land; he was allowed to look onto it from a mountaintop but could not enter in. God does not dismiss or wink at sinful disobedience. Scripture tells us that it is a fearful thing to fall into the hands of an angry God. God is gracious, loving, and kind, but remember, too, that he is Holy God. He is the Alpha and the Omega, the Beginning and the End. We are to have a reverential awe for him. Let's give him and keep him in his rightful place, high and lifted up.

He is to be worshiped.
> He is to be praised.
>> He is to be heralded.
>> He is holy.
>>> He is Lord of all.
>>>> The whole earth is full of his glory.
>>> *Every knee shall bow and every tongue confess* that

Jesus Christ is Lord!

IF I BE LIFTED UP

And I, if I be lifted up from the earth, will draw all men unto me.

John 12:32 (KJV)

Above, the words of Christ spoken in the Gospel of John, foretelling his death.

One of my father's very often quoted statements is "Lift up Christ wherever you go." And he does. Strangers? It matters not. He has loved and walked with Jesus now for so many years, being ninety-six years old, that speaking of Him is just as natural as taking a deep breath for him. And he is right. He is not pushy with his witness. He doesn't badger you. He is loving. He is not condemning. He is humble. He is not judgmental. He simply enjoys talking about Jesus. He loves to brag on Him. He encourages others when they are discouraged. He invites folks to church. He offers sincere prayer. He follows his own advice. He lifts up Christ wherever he goes. You don't have to wonder whose side he is on. He will happily tell you. And I love that about him.

Yes, we can lift up the name of Christ and the Holy Spirit will do the wooing and draw the world to Christ through our witness. We are to plant seeds. God will grow them.

But at Calvary, Christ was literally lifted up from this earth on a cruel rugged cross, and from that cross, he draws all men unto him, still today, more than 2,000 years later. When I imagine this gruesome scene, I can almost hear the dull thud as this heavy and roughly hewn wooden cross sinks into the ground with my Lord hanging from it in pain and agony. Hanging between His own creation, heaven and earth. It took the blood-stained cross of Calvary to save our souls. How he *must* love us!

The cross of Jesus is the bridge that allows the guilty and condemned to safely *cross* over the great gulf of sin that separates us from our God. We can't get to God if we don't come to the cross. Won't you thank Christ that he was willing to lay down his life, for if he had not, we would be forever lost in our sin. So you must "Lift up Christ wherever you go."

Well said, Dad. You can say that again.